OPTIMIZE
PERFORMANCE WITH

Optimize Performance with 5 Dynamics

ISBN-13: 978-1514327920
ISBN-10: 1514327929

First Printing: June 2015

Printed in the United States of America

Table of Contents

PART I: THE BRAIN SEES WHAT IT WANTS TO SEE

1. THE BRAIN SEES WHAT IT WANTS TO SEE 1

    Background 2

    Dynamics + Energy = Success and Satisfaction 3

    The science behind the assessment... 4

    Understanding the 5 Dynamics of a Process....................................... 6

2. UNDERSTANDING YOUR RESULTS.. 9

    Recognizing Energy Intensities & Patterns 11

    Understanding Your Energy Map.. 12

    About Energy Intensity 13

    Self-Reflection Exercise... 15

    How Much Energy can an Individual Have?..................................... 17

    Understanding the 5 Dynamics... 17

3. 5 DYNAMICS AND LEARNING.. 25

    How You Learn Is Shaped by Your Energy 26

    Explore Learning Preferences 27

    Excite Learning Preferences.. 29

    Examine Learning Preferences.. 31

    Execute Learning Preferences... 33

    How each Dynamic shows up in work 36

    Optimizing Your Energy at Work.. 41

    Energy Summary 42

    Energy Patterns Chart.. 43

    Exercise: Applying Energy to Work 46

PART II: IT'S ALL ABOUT RELATIONSHIPS

4. It Takes Two 49

    Tips for Engaging with Other's Energy 50

    Optimizing Short-Term Pair Relationships 58

    Optimizing Longer-Term Relationships for Growth and Influence 58

5. Getting It Done Together 63

    Optimizing Team Performance 64

    Common Imbalances of Energy 68

    Consider Multiple Energy Patterns 68

PART III: OPTIMIZE PERFORMANCE WITH 5 DYNAMICS

6. Practice Makes Perfect 71

    Core Model: The Success–Satisfaction Cycle 72

    Increase Productivity by Reducing Process Loss 73

7. Conclusion 77

APPENDICES

Appendix A: Case Studies 79

Appendix B: 5 Dynamics Foundations 89

Appendix C: Validity & Reliability 103

1. The Brain Sees What It Wants to See

> "In all my research I found people are generally unaware of what drives their impulses, what forces rise up to shape the direction of their thinking and actions time and time again. Only when they are given some insight, can they work to draw on their innate energies."
>
> —W. Michael "Mike" Sturm
> Creator of 5 Dynamics

Key takeaways

Habits exist because:

- The brain sees what it wants to see, based on our most efficient neural pathways,

- People act on those selective perceptions because the brain reuses efficient synapses.

This research underlies the core principles of the 5 Dynamics methodology:

1. Every individual has a preferred process for learning, working and collaborating. When people use this process, success and satisfaction are optimized.

2. Energy preferences are hard-wired tendencies that can be measured.

3. Successful teams engage and align their Energies around the task and each other.

Background

More than forty-five years ago, W. Michael Sturm began observing the patterns of test-takers when he administered assessment instruments to them. He methodically mapped out the process that the test-taker applied to complete the test.

Over time he began to see patterns in these behaviors as well as correlations between the patterns and the test outcomes. The *process* often delivered more information than the test score. For example, Mike noticed that people approached tasks in a particular way based not on what they learned, but on how they naturally went about doing things.

Mike came to understand that there is a **fundamental process underlying how we learn**, create, and accomplish any task—alone or with others.

> **"I didn't develop this to 'fix' people. I developed this to set them free." — Mike Sturm**

Ultimately, Mike developed a process model, coined the **Success/Satisfaction Cycle** model, which eventually became the framework for the 5 Dynamics methodology.

Mike wanted to empower people to recognize where their natural energies (Energetic Preferences) would most comfortably take them, and enable them to use this knowledge to navigate the world successfully and with the least amount of stress.

That's what the 5 Dynamics methodology is all about, in a nutshell.

Dynamics + Energy = Success and Satisfaction

Everyone wants to have success and satisfaction in their work and lives. To do this requires matching your Energy with the Dynamics that will produce the desired results.

Consequently, each of us has specific preferences for applying our Energies to a process. These preferences show up as we work in pairs, teams and organizational groups. When our Energy preferences are aligned with the Dynamic of the work process, there is a greater opportunity for success and satisfaction.

When armed with this information, individuals begin to align their strengths with the tasks at hand. They also begin to comfortably rely on others (and offer support to others) based on their Energetic Preferences.

Basic Definitions

Dynamics: The external phase through which a process is passing.

Energy: The internal power to focus on, engage with, and perform at something over time, without tiring.

Energetic Preferences: The areas where your Energy naturally flows

Success: Quality of a process measured during the Evaluate phase, determined by external criteria related to the output (e.g., cost, time, quality, profit).

Satisfaction: Quality of a process measured during the Evaluate phase, determined by internal criteria related to the actors (e.g., engagement, absence of stress, productivity).

These Energetic Preferences are what the 5 Dynamics assessment measures and is the core of the 5 Dynamics Methodology.

> ### *The assessment is*
>
> *Fast*: 2.5 minutes to complete, instant reports
>
> *Fun*: Reports generated in your Energy style
>
> *Focused*: Make changes that matter
>
> *Fair*: Insights into your strengths without value judgments

The science behind the assessment

Unlike some traditional assessment tools that attempt to label and measure aptitude, competencies, or personality features, 5 Dynamics' assessment is architected on a radically different model.

During his research, Mike became grounded in L.L. Thurstone's law of comparative judgment. This is a statistical technique for measuring how people make decisions along a continuous spectrum when the differences between items can be very small—i.e., "just noticeable differences." It applies to physical phenomena such as weights of objects, as well as to attitudes and opinions. The choice they make is almost invariably right, but when the items are close together, they choose in an unconscious fashion.

In light of Sturm's prior experiences as a social psychologist, this was a fitting statistical approach. At the point of just noticeable differences, a person cannot really think about, verbalize or be aware of what he or she really is doing. This understanding goes far to assure a more valid result.

In a sense, the assessment is neither rationally assembled nor rationally completed. It is based on elicited response of emotions provoked by specific terms. This is not a cognitive form of self-examination. At the same time, people do not behave in a cognitive way because fundamentally they are not rational. People complete the assessment by making neurophysiologic "choices," below their cognitive level.

In terms of current understandings of brain function, the working hypothesis is that when presented with a computer-based assessment containing a selection of words, the brain registers all of the words, but only one of them may, for example, correspond most closely to a person's preferred way of doing things.

The brain is a top-down processor that seeks to recognize what it already knows. Life experiences and positive reinforcement lead to the formation of neural networks that react to the presentation of particular stimulus patterns. Limbic-frontal connections in the brain provide positive emotional valence for a preferred stimulus resulting in an "Ah-ha experience."

The Assessment Does NOT Measure:	It DOES Measure:
<ul><li>Competence</li><li>Intelligence</li><li>Personality</li><li>Personal weakness</li><li>Character traits</li><li>Work ethic</li></ul>	<ul><li>How you focus attention</li><li>Your approach to collaboration</li><li>Your learning style</li><li>Your Energy intensity</li><li>How you focus/work in a process</li></ul>

Thus the subject perceives the socially oriented word as most charged with energy and activates the neural networks for a positive response to socialization. In a broader sense, it is hypothesized that the destinations of these messages control the individual's preferred modalities of perceiving, learning, doing and collaborating.

Discrimination and decision-making are pre-frontal brain functions, but these activities are always colored by the energetic charge that the limbic (emotional) brain provides through direct connections of the limbic system to frontal areas. In order to cut through the noise of additional words presented by Thurstone pairs, the input pathways probably activate limbic pathways to a critical threshold and, hence, achieve an emotional charge that leads to the selection of one word out of the four.

This is not a conscious process although the mind subsequently rationalizes the choice by applying reason or logic to it through post-hoc attributions of value and meaning.

Understanding the 5 Dynamics of a Process

Every person has a preferred way of moving through a process and getting things done, based on their Energies.

For example:

- Some people insist on reading the operating manual first; others will not read manuals at all.

- Some people prefer to work with other people, some prefer to work through other people, and some work around other people.

- Some feel great anxiety about embarking on projects with risky outcomes or unclear procedures; others are highly risk-tolerant.

The Starting Point Assessment identifies the **pattern of focused Energy** which determines a person's preferred way of moving through a process. And virtually everything we do can be broken down into process.

How things get done follows a fundamental, predictable pattern. Each phase, or Dynamic, of a process is distinct and serves a specific purpose: becoming aware of an idea, energizing the idea within one's self or with other people, developing a plan of action, and moving forward to completion.

A Basic Process Model

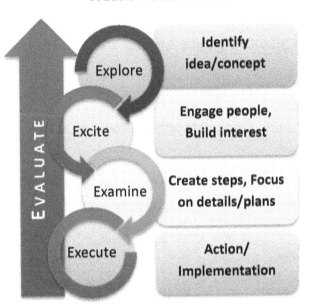

People tend to proceed through these Dynamics in their own **predictable patterns** with respect to time, Energy and focus. These patterns show up in the person's degree of commitment and focused attention to each of these Dynamics.

Our methodology, based on this model of process, is designed to be simple, flexible, and universal. Any user can map his workflow to it and find that the mapping varies very little over time.

5 Dynamics is the only approach that maps the people to the process. When that correlation is clear, understood, and shared, people can move forward rapidly. Using the 5 Dynamics methodology, individuals learn to identify and apply their **unique strengths pattern** to working with others.

- This information helps teams to increase their productivity and reduce friction.

- It provides a common language to focus organizations on building a culture of performance, releasing engagement and innovation.

- People can objectively discuss work, and their contributions, in unambiguous terms that carry no emotional baggage.

- It provides an improved approach for giving insight that you can apply quickly.

Summary

There is a fundamental, predictable pattern underlying how we learn, create, and accomplish any task.

When people understand and recognize their own Energetic preferences, it enables them to navigate the world successfully and with a minimum amount of stress.

The 5 Dynamics methodology is designed to be simple, flexible, and universal; it teaches individuals to identify and apply their unique strengths pattern to any process.

In the next chapter, you'll learn to understand your own unique strengths pattern—your Energetic DNA—as measured by the 5 Dynamics Starting Point assessment.

2. Understanding Your Results

{ "The perfect score is your score!" }

Key takeaways

5 Dynamics is a strengths-based methodology.

- There is no "good" or "bad" score, no "ideal" profile. There is just data.

- Your results are intended to be shared with others, to help everyone value each other's strengths.

- Energy intensity indicates the amount of effort that it will take to focus on a particular Dynamic.

  - More intensity is not better

  - Energies are NOT competencies

  - Energies are NOT labels

Understanding your Energetic preferences is the first step in applying the methodology to your daily work.

- Your 5 Dynamics score is not intended to limit you in any way; instead, it was created to assist you in understanding your natural impulses.
- Your score does not represent what you can and can't do; it simply helps you to see where you focus naturally versus what you might overlook **without awareness.**

So, let's start at the beginning: your individual report. The 5 Dynamics Individual report is great for getting a better **understanding of self**. It gives you a language to express some of your innate processes to the world.

- "Ah, that's why I enjoy that role so much."

- "That explains why I feel tired after a social engagement."

- "I now understand why I am so competitive."

- "I have always had great empathy for others. Now I know why."

- "This explains my lack of tolerance with sloppy work."

The Individual report is actionable immediately in that it gives you a starting point for where to focus, for a **more effective use of your Energy.**

It also helps you to see **where you need to slow down or improve your personal process** to ensure that you are **not skipping over a critical part** of a project, process, or interaction.

- "Seeing my results made it clear to me where I could actually spend more time contributing at work."

- "This made it clear to me that I am connected in the right areas at work."

- "I see how I sometimes get lost in the world of ideas and planning."

- "Wow, no wonder I was driving my team crazy. I went from idea to action and never allowed others to come up to speed by communicating or creating a detailed plan."

Recognizing Energy Intensities & Patterns

Let's look at the four reactions to this SAME presentation.

- Do you recognize yourself here?

- Which of these thoughts do you rarely have?

- Which one(s) do you have most often?

Your answers correlate to your highest Energies. People with different Energies can experience the same presentation very differently.

This is a great example of energy-focus at work.

How often in your group do people talk past each other because of different Energetic preferences?

Have you ever noticed that some people can do something for a long time without getting tired, while another person finds that same work exhausting? This is due to a person's individual Energy pattern to focus on, engage and perform; it is deeply embedded in how your brain responds to its environment.

People naturally prefer to invest high or low amounts of time and Energy at specific points of a process. This focus takes on a consistent, repeated pattern. This is shown in your Energy map in your 5 Dynamics Individual report.

Understanding Your Energy Map

Your Energy Map gives a short version of how you experience energy in each Dynamic. The Energy Map is perhaps the easiest way, at a glance, to understand your own and others' Energetic preferences.

The Dynamic(s) in which you experience the highest Energy intensities indicate where you prefer to learn, work, and collaborate.

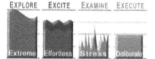 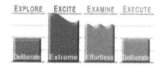 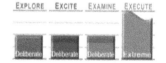

Suspend judgment for a few minutes here

Let's be up-front—some people, especially when they have an Extreme or Stress intensity in one or two areas, jump to the conclusion that they have to "fix" their score. (This is probably due to the sometimes negative connotation that society puts on the ideas of "extreme" and "stress"; the 5 Dynamics methodology uses these terms differently.)

> **There is no "good" or "bad" score, no "ideal" profile.**
> **There is just data.**

5 Dynamics focuses on what you naturally bring to the table, while helping you to discover ways to work through the things that you don't prefer to spend as much time doing. Because 5 Dynamics is strengths-based, your results are intended to be shared, to help everyone value each other's strengths.

Understanding where your Energy is strongest can help you get things done with greater success and satisfaction. Because people usually apply their highest Energies first, this can lead to a mismatch between their Energy and the Dynamic of the process. Learning to match your Energy to the Dynamic helps you understand what roles will make the best use of your Energies.

About Energy Intensity

The 5 Dynamics assessment reveals the predictably repeated pattern of your Energy as you engage with any Dynamic.

Extreme Energy

Indicates an overflow of Energy in this Dynamic. Think of it like a Tsunami wave, moving with great force and direction.

Regardless of where it occurs in the process, this Energy will dominate and can become a liability when it interferes with the need to move through other Dynamics of the cycle.

Effortless Energy

Indicates an easy, comfortable, and efficient level of Energy for this Dynamic. Think of this like a rolling ocean wave, gently moving from the ocean to the shore.

This Energy takes precedence over any other Energy except for Extreme intensity.

Deliberate Energy

Indicates an ability to focus on this Dynamic, but will require some conscious effort. Think of this as flat water: it will take Energy to make your way across it.

This Dynamic can be consciously selected when appropriate for the situation, but it will be less smooth or efficient than Effortless.

Stress Energy

Indicates that being in this Dynamic will be tiring, so people may tend to skip over or move quickly through this Dynamic. Think of this as choppy water, created by a head wind, movement can be accomplished but will take effort and probably tire you out.

It takes the most Energy of any intensity to maintain and is the least comfortable. It causes internal stress when used for prolonged periods of time.

Again, remember that lower Energy is **not a weakness** or indicator of **lack of competency**. In the 5 Dynamics methodology, the Energy intensity indicates the amount of effort that it will take to focus on a particular Dynamic.

- More intensity is not better

- Energies are NOT competencies

- Energies are NOT labels

Based on your personal experience, how would you describe your Energy intensities? (balanced, tilted, even, spiky?)

_____

_____

_____

_____

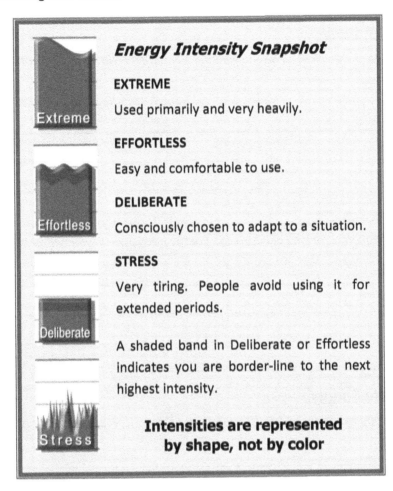

Energy Intensity Snapshot

EXTREME

Used primarily and very heavily.

EFFORTLESS

Easy and comfortable to use.

DELIBERATE

Consciously chosen to adapt to a situation.

STRESS

Very tiring. People avoid using it for extended periods.

A shaded band in Deliberate or Effortless indicates you are border-line to the next highest intensity.

Intensities are represented by shape, not by color

Self-Reflection Exercise

As you look at your Energy Map you will notice that you will have a combination of Energies across the Dynamics. Take a moment and identify how you have experienced each Dynamic or observed another person doing so. Think about behaviors or actions, word choices, or mannerisms you have noticed. Use the next page to record your observations.

Extreme Energy

How have you experienced EXTREME energy intensity—in yourself or others?

_____

_____

_____

_____

Effortless Energy

How have you experienced EFFORTLESS Energy intensity—in yourself or others?

_____

_____

_____

_____

Deliberate Energy

How have you experienced DELIBERATE Energy intensity—in yourself or others?

_____

_____

_____

_____

Stress Energy

How have you experienced STRESS Energy intensity—in yourself or others?

_____

_____

_____

_____

How Much Energy can an Individual Have?

It is natural to wonder if you can have all Extreme or all Stress intensities. Because of the research behind the assessment, it is impossible to have more than one Extreme or Stress Score; however, you can have 0-3 Effortless or 0-4 Deliberate scores. This is where the shaded feature becomes important in distinguishing when you are almost to the next level of intensity.

Extreme	Effortless	Deliberate	Stress
0 or only 1	0 to 3	0 to 4	0 or only 1

Now that you have a clearer understanding of where your own Energies are the strongest, let's go into a little more detail about the Dynamics, or phases, of any process and how your Energies will show up there.

Understanding the 5 Dynamics

Review of the 5 Dynamics process model

All processes, or performance cycles, follow the same basic phases. People naturally prefer to invest high or low amounts of time and Energy at specific points of a process in a consistent, repeated pattern. These patterns manifest themselves in the person's degree of commitment and focused attention to those elements.

Thus, every person has a preferred way of moving through a process and getting things done. As explained in the previous section, your Energetic preferences for getting things done are reflected in your Energy Map.

You can use this knowledge to get things done with greater success and more happiness.

The whole big idea is to match the Energies with the Dynamics. You need one eye on the work—the Dynamics—and the other on the people, and how they are applying themselves—their Energies.

How It Works

All individuals and teams use a common process in everything they do, individually or together.

2. The **idea** or **awareness** is **energized, radiated and championed** to advance it toward planning.

3. The **energized idea** is then analyzed and developed into **a detailed plan with procedures, standards and timelines**.

1. Every initiative starts with an **awareness**, an **idea** or a **concept**.

4. All tasks from the **plan** are **actively completed** with **Energy** and **awareness**; all involved are held accountable.

5. The Cycle is evaluated by asking if it has been completed with **success and satisfaction**.

1 Explore   2 Excite   3 Examine   4 Execute   5 Evaluate

All of us are tempted, without awareness, to apply our highest Energies first and most, regardless of whether they are called for. Sometimes we overdo an Energy.

We'd like to think that we have the right proportion of Energies, naturally, all the time, and that we always apply them in the best sequence. The truth is that we have to be very conscious of what a situation needs, and what people are bringing to it. If you can keep this close to front of mind all the time, you are really using what you are learning about the 5 Dynamics methodology.

To that end, let's look more closely at each of these five Dynamics.

Explore

Everything we do must begin with an idea. How much of a charge do you get from living in the in the world of ideas? This means exploring the future, thinking about new and creative ways of putting things together, or considering options for long periods of time.

People who prefer to work with ideas, alternatives, and conceptual creativity have high intensity in Explore. This is the strategic thinking-oriented phase of any process.

Do you see yourself in any of the following?

- "I enjoy putting my mark on an idea."
- "I am always asking, 'How?' or 'What if...?'"
- "I frequently try to find connections between ideas, knowledge, and possibilities."
- "I want to understand the Big Picture before going forward."

How do you personally experience the first Dynamic, Explore? Is your Energy higher or lower in this Dynamic?

_____

_____

What is required to effectively move into and out of the Explore Dynamic?

_____

_____

What difference do you experience, if any, in your Explore Energy when you are moving through a process solo versus working with others?

_____

_____

Excite

The work of Excite, the second Dynamic, is to generate and focus the Energy of the ideas and move them into planning and action.

This phase is about getting one's self and others excited and on board. It's all about communicating and energizing—getting the word out, talking about the ideas, getting others involved, and gaining others' commitment. It's about sharing one's enthusiasm.

Do you see yourself in any of the following?
- "I enjoy talking with others early on about a new idea."
- "I like to get others engaged in moving an idea forward."
- "I particularly enjoy doing things in groups."

How do you personally experience the second Dynamic, Excite? Is your Energy higher or lower in this Dynamic?

_____

_____

What is required to effectively move into and out of the Excite Dynamic?

_____

_____

What differences do you experience, if any, in your Excite Energy when you are moving through a process solo versus working with others?

_____

_____

Examine

We might think of Examine, the third Dynamic, as the analytical or due diligence part of the cycle.

In this Dynamic a person deconstructs the ideas; makes plans; puts processes in place; conducts research and analysis; establishes measurements, standards, and rules; sets procedures and timelines.

In this Dynamic a person: develops the planning structure that will support results, anticipates obstacles, and identifies contingencies.

Do you see yourself in any of the following?

- "I enjoy the data and detailed parts of planning."
- "I like to create procedures and roadmaps for getting things accomplished."
- "I enjoying finding mistakes and working with data."

How do you personally experience the third Dynamic, Examine? Is your Energy higher or lower in this Dynamic?

_____

_____

What is required to effectively move into and out of the Examine Dynamic?

_____

_____

What differences do you experience, if any, in your Examine Energy when you are moving through a process solo versus working with others?

_____

_____

Execute

The fourth Dynamic, Execute, is the mobilization stage in which everyone is charged with completing the necessary tasks defined by the plan.

It's about getting one's self and others into focused, accountable action. It's also about moving forward within the identified structures and systems to get things done within deadlines. People receive their assignments, embark on tasks, and move to completion.

Do you see yourself in any of the following?
- "I can't wait to get things done so I can feel the pleasure that comes from completing something."
- "I like being responsible for getting things done against a deadline."
- "I enjoy holding others accountable for accomplishing goals."

How do you personally experience the fourth Dynamic, Execute? Is your Energy higher or lower in this Dynamic?

_____

_____

What is required to effectively move into and out of the Execute Dynamic?

_____

_____

What differences do you experience, if any, in your Execute Energy when you are moving through a process solo versus working with others?

_____

_____

Evaluate

The fifth Dynamic of the 5 Dynamics model is called Evaluate. It is at this point that you think about the entire preceding cycle from two perspectives: internal and external.

Satisfaction is based on your own internal experience.
- Were you satisfied with the outcome?
- Did you feel good about your accomplishment and how you moved through each phase of the process?
- Did you like working with others?

Success is based on external metrics.
- Did you meet your goals?
- Did you deliver the expected results?
- Did you accomplish your tasks on time and within budget?

How do you personally experience the fifth Dynamic, Evaluate?

_____

_____

How might your high Energy Dynamic(s) influence your evaluation of a process?

_____

_____

How might your individual evaluation of a process differ from those of other people with whom you are working?

_____

_____

More about Success and Satisfaction

We have said that every organizational member has specific preferences for applying his or her Energies to a process. These preferences translate to any learning, working or collaborative endeavor.

An individual's process preferences represent innate strengths that can be distinguished from intellectual aptitude, character traits, technical and interpersonal competencies, and personality.

When a person's process-strengths and preferences are aligned with job tasks and a role on a team, the predictable outcomes are **Success** (externally measured) and **Satisfaction** (internally experienced).

Both the individual and the organization establish measurable success criteria. When the criteria of both are well aligned, individual success directly translates to organizational success. Mutual satisfaction is the natural result.

Where there is good alignment, then greater employee engagement, increased customer satisfaction, heightened trust and reduced individual and organizational stress also appear as benefits.

Summary

Understanding how your Energetic preferences show up during the Dynamics of any process is the first step in applying the 5 Dynamics methodology to your daily work. In the next chapter, we will discover how these Energetic preferences also line up with how you prefer to learn new information.

Remember, your 5 Dynamics score is not intended to limit you in any way. Instead, it was created to assist you in understanding your natural impulses. Your score does not represent what you can and can't do; it simply helps you to see where you focus naturally versus what you might overlook without awareness.

As Mike Sturm, creator of the 5 Dynamics Methodology often stated, "I didn't create this to change you. I created this to set you free.

3. 5 Dynamics and Learning

{
"5 Dynamics helps individuals understand how they learn.

With this simple, yet profound information, people are able to optimize how they work and how they collaborate."
}

Key takeaways

Our Energetic Preferences are clearly demonstrated in how we learn.

- How you take in information, make sense of the environment and find value is shaped by your Energy pattern.

- The location of your highest Energies (Effortless or Extreme) indicates the learning preferences to which you will be most drawn, the ones with which you will be most comfortable.

- Learning preferences can be mapped to the process model.

- Ultimately, learning preferences can be used to best engage others in presentations and interactions.

How we work and collaborate directly correlates to how we learn.

- Understanding how your Energies show up in the Dynamics of work cycles allows you to optimize your performance based on your strengths.

- This same principle can be applied to interacting with others.

The Evaluate Dynamics shouldn't be overlooked or undervalued.

- Most people evaluate their success and satisfaction from the perspective of their highest Energies.

- Giving equal time to the evaluation of the other Dynamics is potentially where you have the greatest opportunity for growth.

How You Learn Is Shaped by Your Energy

Think back to when you were in grade school. Were you the student that needed to see the big picture first before the details made sense? Maybe you were the kid who consistently finished your assignment first and ended up grading a lot of papers for the teachers. Maybe you were the kid who got in trouble for being too wiggly and talking too much, or perhaps you were the kid who set the curve in the math classes as logical, fact-based concepts came easily to you.

Your Energetic preferences showed up early in life and will stay with you for the remainder of your life. So, let's take a minute to look at learning styles.

As discussed in the last chapter, your 5 Dynamics results show you the predictably repeated pattern of your Energy as you engage with any Dynamic. The more you understand this pattern, the easier it will be to mobilize yourself to move through all 5 Dynamics.

To do this requires understanding your pattern and the patterns of others. When you are able to identify what Energy intensity you are bringing to the Dynamic, and what others are contributing then you will be able to allocate work roles, tasks and accountabilities in a way that best matches the available Energies.

The best way to think about how to apply your Energy is to think about how you learn: how you take in information, make sense of the environment and find value.

Your learning preferences are shaped by your Energy pattern. The location of your highest Energies (Effortless or Extreme) indicates the learning preferences to which you will be most drawn, the ones with which you will be most comfortable.

For example, if you have high Energy in Explore, you will be interested in looking at the future implications of a trend or event. You will think out of the box and come up with seemingly unconnected ways of approaching a topic.

Your Energy Map will show you in which Dynamics you have the highest Energy. On the following pages you will find summaries of how each learning style is exhibited. While each Energy is discussed independently, keep in mind that your unique combination of Energies may make certain learning characteristics more, or less, relevant to you.

Explore Learning Preferences

People with high Energy in
Explore

• Creating visions and new ideas	"I enjoy coming up with the big idea."
• Solving problems creatively	
• Seeing future implications	"I am always asking, 'How?' or 'What if...?'"
• Being aware of feelings and undercurrents	"I frequently try to find connections between ideas, knowledge, and possibilities."
• Connecting the seemingly unconnected	
	"I want to understand the Big Picture before going forward."

If you have high Explore Energy, you have an unusual learning style seldom accommodated by traditional teaching methods. You are a **conceptual thinker** who must see the big picture before anything begins to make real sense. You are always unconsciously asking the question, "How?"

You are searching for the **underlying process** that **connects** everything into a whole that makes sense to you.

Without the "How?" and its conceptual whole, you have inconsistent and seemingly scattered ways to tie together theories, facts, and pertinent information. But once that whole is created, you can memorize facts by placing them into a framework.

Besides being the most creative and aware thinkers, you are the most independent of thinkers and learners. Not only can you connect disparate facts and information into unified concepts, but you also can generate a multitude of optional thoughts to solve problems or look at a situation in novel ways.

In other words, you reinvent how material is presented and adapt it to your way of seeing things. That's why you like to go off by yourself for an "incubation period" to learn and absorb what's just been presented.

You relate best to **analogies** and **multiple ways of presenting ideas and facts**. It's through these stories and differences that you can begin to integrate what's being taught into you learning process. You are an **associative learner**.

Visuals, graphics, and the use of a multitude of colors for differentiating facts and their concepts help to reinforce your learning.

You also enjoy group discussions as another way of having material presented. It can be particularly helpful to your learning process if a visual and verbal summary is created at the end.

How do you experience learning from the Explore perspective?

_____

_____

_____

What supports Explore Learning?

_____

_____

_____

Excite Learning Preferences

People with high Energy in
Excite

• Sharing ideas and feelings	"I enjoy talking with others early on about a new idea."
• Mobilizing people to move ideas forward	"I like to get others engaged in moving an idea forward."
• Being entertaining and dramatic	
• Getting "the word" out to build engagement	"I particularly enjoy doing things in groups."

If you have high Excite Energy, you are a **social** learner and are always unconsciously asking the question, "Who?"

You relate to information through personal stories, personal implications to yourself and others, and anecdotes. You are not a blank-slate learner who memorizes information and regurgitates it later.

Positive encouragement and reinforcement delivered in a personal manner can motivate you to accept and adapt to any criticisms or corrections needed. In fact, you **love** to be praised and positively singled out in a group.

Visuals with colors to separate thoughts and **informational relationships** are very helpful to your learning process.

When memorization was required in school settings, you would have benefited from creating rhymes or songs about material. (The more absurd and humorous these memory tools, the easier it would be for you to learn.)

Now, in work settings, you may be less conversant with factual data and more likely to "shoot from the hip" or "decide from the gut."

You immediately have an innate need to **TALK** about, or talk through anything being taught. That's because you learn best by orally repeating what has just been presented and participating in an ongoing, corrective dialogue about it.

Whatever is being taught to you will be **personally** adapted and used for future interactive exchange. The parts of your brain that facilitate long-term memory are highly connected to the auditory and socially-oriented parts.

You are a **great responder** to, but perhaps **not a great listener** to, what is being stated.

Because you are an intuitive and interactive learner, you have a difficult time sticking to a schedule or attending to something that is presented only in a logical manner. If the presenter can make learning "FUN!" then you will flourish.

How do you experience learning from the Excite perspective?

_____

_____

_____

What supports Excite Learning?

_____

_____

_____

Examine Learning Preferences

<table>
<tr><td colspan="2" align="center">*People with high Energy in*
Examine</td></tr>
<tr>
<td>

- Organizing and creating structure and systems

- Making realistic timelines, schedules and deadlines

- Researching, investigating, collecting data, adjusting interdependencies

- Exposing flaws and correcting mistakes, anticipating obstacles

</td>
<td>

"I enjoy the data and detailed parts of planning."

"I like to create procedures and roadmaps for getting things accomplished."

"I enjoying finding mistakes and working with data."

</td>
</tr>
</table>

1. If you have high Energy in Examine, you constantly ask the question, "Why?"

2. You critically look for inconsistencies or errors that people might make

3. You learn by:

   a. Logic / Cause and effect

   b. Hypothesis and conclusion

   c. Facts / Linear sequences

4. Your attitude and approach:

   a. Serious / Focused

   b. No tolerance for imprecision or loose language

   c. Everything stated must be defensible; the more accurate, the better

   d. Punctual / Efficient

5. You learn best:

   a. In a traditional classroom setting

   b. When information is presented logically and sequentially

    i. In a consistent format and filled with pertinent, factual information that backs up any assumptions and theories presented.

    ii. With little use of color

6. You are also characterized by

    a. Excellent listening skills

    b. Good verbal memory

To expand briefly on the outline above, you enjoy facts and do best with linear, logical sequences. Because of this, compared to other learners, you are most comfortable and successful in a traditional classroom setting using traditional teaching methods.

To get the most value from a learning experience, you expect, and even demand, teachers or facilitators:

- Show up on time and make efficient use of time during the session,
- Be serious about the material,
- Avoid too much levity or personal anecdotes,
- Stay focused on the topic until it is completed,
- Present information in a logical and sequential order.

How do you experience learning from the Examine perspective?

_____

_____

_____

What supports Examine Learning?

_____

_____

_____

Execute Learning Preferences

People with high Energy in
Execute

• Holding yourself and others accountable for results	"I can't wait to get things done so I can feel the pleasure that comes from completing something."
• Moving forward, beyond obstacles	"I like being responsible for getting things done against a deadline."
• Using structures and systems to get things done	
• Giving and getting rewards for accomplishments	"I enjoy holding others accountable for accomplishing goals."

If you have high Energy in Execute, you:

- **Ask "What?"** "What's the purpose? What's the point? What's my immediate assignment? What can I do to better learn the material?"

- Look first for objectives, expectations and criteria, and clearly delineated levels for success

- Categorize all materials

- Thrive on challenges!

- Focus on pragmatic, practical applications of information

- Learn best from kinetic, action-oriented activities

- Respect efficiency, punctuality

- Agree that "less is more"; prefer bullet points over exposition

- Would rather choose from fewer, quality options

- Appreciate honest criticism, followed by immediate instruction

To expand on a few of the previous points:

Thrive on challenges! You respond extremely well in a learning environment that is competitive and pushes your limits. When challenged by someone you respect, you'll work until exhausted.

Focus on the pragmatic. You "register" material when you understand a practical application for it. Unless you also have high Explore Energy, you will be turned off by theory.

Respect efficiency, punctuality. These are attributes you require of yourself and respect in others. You prefer to express ideas in a succinct way and to finish every task in the least amount of time. You quickly can become impatient with confusion, tardiness and too many choices.

Appreciate honest criticism. You prefer criticism followed by immediate instruction of what to do to correct a problem or situation.

How do you experience learning from the Execute perspective?

_____

_____

_____

What supports Execute Learning?

• Room to finish   • Immediate feedback   • Clarity/recognition about winning

_____

_____

_____

What if I have all 4 Deliberate Energies?

Congratulations! You have the most unique Energy pattern and perhaps the most versatile.

You are a well-balanced learner. Depending on the assignment/task to be accomplished, you easily can be creative and option-oriented or logical and sequentially focused.

You can learn from almost any person or method because you readily adapt to any style of presentation. However, you probably succeed best in a traditional classroom setting.

You respect people who are punctual, demand punctuality, and follow through on what you say you will do. You will attempt to accomplish whatever is expected of you to become successful.

You are a responsible learner; therefore, if you aren't succeeding, it's not because you aren't doing your best. It probably means you are lacking some prerequisite skills or need some individual assistance.

You can be patient and attentive. You are an above-average listener. Whether you must attend to verbal or nonverbal listening cues makes no difference.

You will work diligently at memorizing any material you are expected to know. Also, you will work independently to acquire the skills you lack to accomplish any expected objectives.

You enjoy teaching and learning methods that have clear expectations, predictable consequences and constant rhythms. Inconsistent extremes in teaching methods and presentations may create distress for you.

Material is best structured logically and sequentially so that you develop the topic and material initially introduced and outlined.

Now that you are aware of the 5 Dynamics' learning preferences, think about how to connect with others in their preferred styles. Influence is a hot topic at the moment. The best way to influence another person is to connect with them in the way with which they are most comfortable—empathetic communication goes a long way. If you are mindful of their preferences and they are mindful of yours, you will both be happier with the partnership.

Chapter 5, beginning on page 49, includes advice on how to engage others, based on their own learning preferences, for better communication and outcomes.

How each Dynamic shows up in work

Just as your preferred way of learning is tied to your Energetic preferences, so is your preferred way of getting things done. Applying this knowledge allows you and your team to optimize how you work and collaborate with each other.

Explore at Work

With high **Explore Energy**, everything begins with a concept, an awareness, an idea—a focus on thinking about the future, being interested in novel ways of putting things together.

EXPLORE – Ideas

- Identifying the awareness, idea, concept
- Creating visions and new ideas
- Seeing future implications
- Connecting seemingly unconnected elements

People who have high Energy in this Dynamic prefer to work with generating ideas and alternatives. Their approach is to look for the overarching theme and then consider many options at once.

Excite at Work

Excite Energy is focused on connecting people to ideas, helping refine and focus the idea so others can engage with it.

EXCITE – People

- Communicating and engaging others to get involved
- Sharing ideas and feelings
- Generating excitement
- Getting the word out

People with high Energy in this Dynamics use rapid input to sharpen the focus and hone the idea for planning.

The interest is about communicating and energizing—getting the word out, talking about the ideas, getting others involved, and gaining others' commitment. It's about sharing one's enthusiasm.

Examine at Work

Examine Energy brings the analytical mindset to the situation.

In this Dynamic plans are made; processes are created and put in place; research and analyses are conducted; measurements, standards, and rules are designated; procedures and timelines are established.

EXAMINE – Plan

- Analyzing and solving problems with data
- Developing structures and systems that will support results
- Making realistic steps, timelines, adjusting sequence
- Exposing flaws and correcting mistakes

People with high Energy in this Dynamic do well at developing the structures which will support results, anticipate obstacles, and identify contingencies.

Execute at Work

Execute Energy focuses on mobilizing for completion of the plan. Attention is directed toward getting into focus and finishing what you set out to do.

This is the phase where people hold themselves and others accountable for deadlines and results.

EXECUTE – Action

- Mobilizing to finish what you set out to do
- Demanding accountability and results
- Moving forward not matter what is in the way
- Giving and getting rewards for accomplishments

Those with high Execute Energy move projects forward within the identified structures and systems to get things done. People receive their assignments, embark on tasks, and move to completion.

Evaluate at Work

Evaluate is the phase where you think about the entire cycle from two perspectives—success and satisfaction. Effective Evaluation takes into account all Dynamics.

We do not measure the fifth Dynamic, because it is different for every process. The focus of this Dynamic is look at each of the other four Dynamics and to ask how successful and satisfied were you at moving through each of the Dynamics.

> ## EVALUATE
> ### Review/Learn
>
> Determining how successful and satisfied were you with the results in each Dynamic.
>
> **Success Evaluation**
> - How well did you meet the overall goals?
> - How successful were you based on metrics, standards, outcomes (e.g., revenue targets, on-time, quality, profit margin, customer satisfaction)?
>
> **Satisfaction Evaluation**
> - How did you feel about your accomplishment?
> - How smoothly did you move through each phase of the process?
> - How well did you work with others' energies?

It is important to evaluate each Dynamic to learn and improve focus.

Explore

How creative were you? How well did you grasp the big picture?

Excite

How energized were you and others about the idea?

Examine

What was the quality of the data and planning?

Execute

How effectively and efficiently were your goals met?

Possible Trap

Most people evaluate their success and satisfaction from the perspective of their highest Energies. While this is a natural response to our Energetic preferences, you have to take care not to ignore the other Dynamics—this is potentially where you have the greatest opportunity for growth.

For example, if you have high Energy in Examine you will look primarily at the quality of the data/analysis and the thoroughness of the planning. However, if you ignore evaluation of the Explore Dynamic, then you may not realize that a major solution to the problem, which could have significantly improved outcomes, was never even considered.

> "With awareness during the Evaluate Dynamic, you can choose to make behavioral changes to improve your own process, your group process, and/or your business process."

What gets measured gets attended to. Evaluate is arguably the most important part of the methodology; however, because it is not measurable by the assessment, people tend to forget about it. Do not let this happen!

In truth, Evaluate is where most of the improvement occurs. The preceding Dynamics are just the proving grounds where people can do something right or not right. The proof resides in the results. They are outcomes, and hostages to the preceding process.

Optimizing Your Energy at Work

<u>Review the Energy Summary</u>

On the next page you will see the Energies—Explore, Excite, Examine, Execute—explained by how those with high Energy in each tend to focus.

Locate your highest Energy(s) and read down the column for that Energy. If you have two or three Effortless, then look at the Energy Patterns Chart beginning on page 43 to see how those Energies show up when combined.

Which words or phrases stood out for you?

_____

_____

_____

_____

_____

_____

Energy Summary

HOW THOSE HIGH IN THIS ENERGY PERCEIVE THE WORLD:

Explore

Wants to know "How?"

Prefers to "Live in the Future"

High interest in creative concepts and causes

Intuitive, non-linear, and independent thinking

Seeks harmony by unifying people and ideas

Sees patterns and connections: Big Picture thinker

Considers multiple options, feelings, and reasons

Idealist; visionary; anti-authoritarian

Excite

Wants to know "Who?

Prefers to "Live In The Now"

High interest in people and places

Spontaneous and intuitive; focus shifts rapidly

Seeks synergy through interaction and play

Sees world through people, relationships, stories, and inspiration

Charming and adaptable; a "people"-person

Persuasive optimist

Examine

Wants to know "Why?"

Prefers the past

High interest in details and facts backed by hard data

Intense ability to focus; thinking is rigorous and thorough

Seeks "Truth" through validation of data

Sees world through logic, facts, and data. "What has worked well in the past?"

Seemingly distant and impersonal; not expressive but listens acutely

Skeptic

Execute

Wants to know "What?"

Prefers the present but with measurable time-frames

High interest in action and objects

Concrete pragmatic thinking, common sense-limited options

Seeks results through challenge, competition, and confrontation

Sees concrete, pragmatic tactics, goals, and results

Enacting, moving, and driving.

Authoritative

Energy Patterns Chart

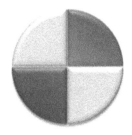

2	3
1	4

1. Explore   3. Examine
2. Excite   4. Execute

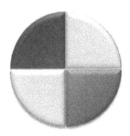

Explore-Examine: This pattern prefers to think more than act, but moves very easily between two ways of thinking: flexible/creative vs. orderly/rational. Such people spend deceptively large amounts of energy quietly working things through in their heads. People with this pattern are quiet, gentle, and "thoughtful" in both senses of the word.

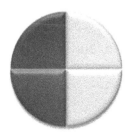

Excite-Execute: Very action-oriented, almost hyperactive. This pattern is constantly busy doing *something*—talking or doing. People with this pattern appear to be highly empowered in almost everything they attempt. They give the appearance of being highly effective in action since they tend to respond quickly as they think.

Explore-Excite: Flexible ways of thinking (intuition, empathy, integration, service, and risk) are their keys to action. People with this pattern are noted for being creative, artistic and trend-setting futuristic thinkers. Planning, logic, and sequencing are not usually part of their innate everyday repertoire. They are energized by the interplay between ideas and people.

Examine-Execute: People with this Energy-focus pattern can plan and act with equal ease. However, they do so by using more of the order-based ways of thinking (logical, linear, detailed, punctual and verbal) rather than the more flexible approaches. They have a high need for control. They are energized by the interplay between data and results.

Excite-Examine: These people may be very detailed, sequential and focused. Just as easily, they unknowingly switch to fun-loving, spontaneous, and flexible. This person is at ease in both seemingly opposing modes. No other pattern moves between opposites this way, and it is difficult to predict which Energy-focus you will see.

Explore-Execute: Individuals with this pattern are independent and entrepreneurial. They are usually workaholics who see the Big Picture and actively pursue what they want. This is the most intense of all the combinations. They often follow goals without first inviting other people along, and do not naturally create a detailed plan. Burn-out is a risk.

Explore-Excite-Examine: This pattern strongly prefers to avoid conflict. Frequently people with this rare score show great skill in subtly persuading other people to do the actual implementation. They can be inspiring leaders with a creative fire and analytic insights. Follow-through is either learned behavior or is delegated.

Explore-Excite-Execute: Frequently a whirlwind of activities and projects. These often charismatic people are constantly in motion, seeing possibilities, inspiring people and promoting action; they can hit the wall unless they prioritize the innumerable possibilities they can devise.

Explore-Examine-Execute: Highly competent and self-reliant, this pattern leads by quiet example. Usually serious, ambitious, and reserved, these people tend to limit warm personal relationships at work, while setting high standards for effort and achievement. Expect encouragement but no team hugs.

Excite-Examine-Execute: This pattern is hard-working, empowered and empowering, happily driving others toward lofty goals, generally with success. These people may feel uncomfortable only at the beginning, chaotic, early stages of a project. Providing a clear early vision and direction may be essential; thereafter, they enjoy building a team and producing excellent results.

Exercise: Applying Energy to Work

Think about a project or process you are engaged with, or recently completed. In the space below:

1. List the major tasks or deliverables required in the process.

2. Which Dynamics were particularly important to each task? Score them in the shaded columns: 3 = "a lot"; 1 = "some"; 0 = "none"

3. Consider your own Energy in those Dynamics. How do you experience it? What did you notice about your colleagues in those Dynamics? With what you have been learning, could you contemplate any improvements the next time you do something like this?

	Task or Deliverable	Explore	Excite	Examine	Execute	Notes
1						
2						
3						
4						
5						
6						
7						
8						
9						
10						

Energetic Awareness

After completing the exercise on the previous page, think about how you would answer these questions.

1. What phases of the process held your focus the most? Why?

2. Where did you have the least focus? Why?

3. How did your actions and outcomes reflect these differences?

4. At the point of completion of the process, how did you feel about it?

5. What adjustments did you make if any?

Summary

Your highest Energies indicate the learning preferences to which you will be most drawn and most comfortable.

Likewise, your preferred way of getting things done is also tied to your Energetic preferences.

Applying this knowledge allows you to optimize how you work and collaborate with others.

When moving through the Dynamics of any process, do not overlook the 5th Dynamic, Evaluate, as this is where most of your improvement occurs.

In Part II, we'll explore how to apply 5 Dynamics to the relationships around you, both in pairs and in teams.

4. It Takes Two

{
"Appreciation is a wonderful thing. It makes what is
excellent in others belong to us as well."

— Voltaire
}

Key takeaways

5 Dynamics is a strengths-based methodology.

- Lower Energy is not a weakness or indicator of lack of competency.

- In the 5 Dynamics methodology, the Energy intensity indicates the amount of effort that it will take to focus on a particular Dynamic.

  - More intensity is not better

  - Energies are NOT competencies

  - Energies are NOT labels

Understanding another's Energetic preferences allows you to engage them more effectively.

- When your Energies match those of another person, interaction comes naturally.

- When your Energies differ from those of another, a conscious effort and simple strategy can produce the same results.

5 Dynamics can be used to optimize your working relationships.

Tips for Engaging with Other's Energy

When working with someone whose highest Energy is the same as yours, you'll usually find that interaction comes naturally, as you both learn and communicate using the same strategies. But how do you go about engaging someone whose Energy is different from yours?

Where to Start

- Start with any Effortless or Extreme Energy

- If Execute is one of multiple Effortless Energies, then start there

How to Engage Those with Execute Energy

EXECUTE – Action

Their Energy intensity **increases** when they must:

- Get it done!
- Have direct power to finish
- Keep score
- Lead and shape groups for action
- Challenge and activate; push hard for results
- Demand action and accountability

Their Energy intensity **decreases** when they must:

- Deal with ideas and not action
- Tolerate too many options
- Endure indecision or delays
- Resist the urge to take command of the outcome
- Demonstrate patience over prolonged periods
- Slow down
- Open up, lighten up, loosen up
- Put people-concerns first and results second

1. **Help them understand "What?" up front.** "What's the purpose? What's the point? What's my immediate task? What can I do to better get this done?"

    Immediately present goals, objectives, and expectations in all meetings. For projects and evaluations, also provide clearly delineated levels for success: "Here is the finish line, and here's what we need to do to get there."

2. **Be clear, logical, and practical in all interactions.** As pragmatists, they prefer application over theory. Unless they also have high Explore Energy, they will be turned off by theory and become impatient. As kinetic, action-oriented learners, they "register" material when they understand a practical application for it.

3. **Dare them to be more successful and push them to their limits.** They thrive on challenges and respond extremely well in a competitive environment. When challenged by someone they respect, they'll work until exhausted.

    As they are always looking to improve, give clear direction and lots of direct feedback. They prefer criticism followed by immediate suggestions of what to do to correct a problem or situation.

4. **Be on time and organized.** Efficiency, punctuality and conciseness are attributes they require of themselves and respect in others. Therefore, during meetings, be on time and be organized; stay on topic as digression will create boredom, impatience and even anger.

    Keep examples and alternatives down to two, maybe three at most. At the end of a meeting, summarize and make requests for their evaluation.

5. **"Less is more."** They prefer to express ideas in a succinct way and to finish every task in the least amount of time. They thrive on bullet points and brevity. They tend to categorize all materials presented into logical boxes that can be easily retrieved from memory.

How to Engage Those with Explore Energy

EXPLORE – Ideas

Their Energy intensity <u>increases</u> when they must:

- Deepen understanding of possibilities and innovative solutions
- Broaden the scope
- Create something new that unites all the people and multiple elements
- Promote inclusiveness, unity and cooperation
- Create innovative solutions

Their Energy intensity <u>decreases</u> when they must:

- Deal with limitations, rules, and restrictions
- Complete tasks immediately
- Hold themselves back from over-commitment
- Take decisive actions over prolonged periods
- Make tough decisions, prioritize or say "no"
- Set firm and consistent interpersonal boundaries
- Resist the urge to take things personally
- Do things conventionally

1. **Introduce all new topics with the Big Picture.** They are conceptual thinkers who must see the forest before the trees. They are always unconsciously asking the questions, "How?" and "What if...?"

2. **Connect each topic to the benefit of the project.** Without the Big Picture, they have inconsistent and seemingly scattered ways to tie together theories, facts, and pertinent information. But once that "whole strategy" is created, they can memorize facts by placing them into a framework.

3. **Use analogies or stories.** They relate best to analogies and multiple ways of presenting ideas and facts. As associative learners, it's through stories and differences that they begin to integrate new information into the whole.

4. **When appropriate, make time for short but open discussions.** They are creative, aware and independent thinkers; they can connect disparate facts and information into unified concepts and also can generate many options to solve problems or look at a situation in novel ways.

5. **Allow them an "incubation period."** As conceptual thinkers, they reinvent how material is presented to them and adapt it to their way of seeing things. That's why they like to go off by themselves for a time to learn and absorb what's just been presented. Whenever possible, don't go "by the book"; instead, help them reach conclusions through discovery.

6. **Use colorful, graphically vibrant visual aids.** It can be particularly helpful to add a visual and verbal summary at the end. They also enjoy small-group discussions to assimilate new information.

7. **Hold them accountable for their time.** They are sometimes not as aware of time as others. During a formal process/project, write a personal contact committing each other to punctuality, clear deadlines and outcomes.

8. **Be positive and specific in your criticisms.**

How to Engage Those with Excite Energy

EXCITE – People
Their Energy intensity <u>increases</u> when they must: • Raise energy and gather power • Acknowledge strengths and capacities of others • Inject fun and align people for action • Create fun, productive interactions and teamwork • Weave people together Their Energy intensity <u>decreases</u> when they must: • Ignore distractions • Stay disciplined and serious • Work alone, or cannot delegate to others • Express ideas in only a few words • Wait before committing to a task • Stay out of the spotlight • Deal with others' negativity • Maintain a distance from people for a long time

1. **Use personal stories and anecdotes**; spell out the implications to themselves and others. They are social engagers and are always unconsciously asking the question, "Who?"

2. **Allow them time to talk.** Such people immediately have an innate need to talk about, or talk through anything being presented. That's because they

learn best by orally repeating what has just been presented and participating in an ongoing, collaborative dialogue about it.

3. **Make meetings fun!** They are not blank-slate learners who memorize information and regurgitate it later, so avoid dry facts and data. Instead, set a fast pace with varied activities, intuitive and interactive in nature. As much as possible, sustain continuous dialogue with them so that what you are presenting stays fresh and memorable.

4. **Create and stick to a schedule.** Because they are intuitive and interactive, they have a difficult time sticking to a schedule or attending to something that is presented only in a logical manner. Create an organized schedule, but if necessary, conceal the structure.

5. **Keep it personal and positive.** Positive encouragement and reinforcement delivered in a personal manner can motivate these members to accept and adapt to any criticisms or corrections needed. In fact, they love to be praised and positively singled out in a group. Offer reinforcement to motivate any adaptation you recommend. Refer to specific actions that will be different because of your interaction.

6. **Check their understanding.** They are great responders to, but not great listeners to, what is being stated. Ask indirect questions to confirm learning and insure internalization of ideas.

7. **Keep them engaged.** Visuals with colors to separate thoughts and informational relationships are very helpful to their engagement process. Casually ask stimulating and personal questions for engagement.

How to Engage Those with Examine Energy

EXAMINE – Plan

Their Energy intensity <u>increases</u> when they must:

- Look at situations thoroughly

- Promote caution and rigor

- Study what's possible or impossible with data; find errors

- Develop plans, rules, procedures and timelines

- Perform "reality" checks

Their Energy intensity <u>decreases</u> when they must:

- Produce while feeling rushed or pushed

- Show more flexibility over prolonged periods

- Outwardly demonstrate passion and personal concern

- Take risks without data, or tolerate errors/sloppiness

- Identify patterns and the Big Picture

- Envision optimistic outcomes without supporting data

- Personally acknowledge internal needs of self and others

- Let go and move on

1. **Don't take it personally.** To begin with, always remember that they are unconsciously asking the question, "Why?" and are critically looking for any inconsistencies or errors that you might make. They have almost no tolerance for imprecision or loose language; everything stated must be defensible, and the more accurate, the better.

2. **Shift your thinking.** Such people learn by logic: cause and effect, hypothesis and conclusion. They enjoy facts and do best with linear logical sequences. Information presented should be logical and sequential in format and filled with pertinent, factual information that backs up any assumptions and theories presented.

3. **Plan ahead.** Plan your presentation and avoid improvisation. Create and adhere to an outline that is clear and specific.

4. **Be on time.** Make sure you are punctual, precise, and prepared. Punctuality and efficient use of time are a must. If you are late, ill prepared, or illogical it will devalue the conversation/presentation/session.

5. **Present information in a logical, consistent order.** State what you will do. Use data and facts to back up all your main points, theories, and opinions. Summarize what you are able to provide.

6. **Always follow up.** Ask questions for feedback. Ask for an evaluation of each experience. Give direct, concise feedback when appropriate.

7. **Remain serious and thoughtful.** They enjoy engaging with people who are serious about the material. You must stay focused on the topic until it is completed. An anecdote or joke here and there may help, but too much levity can lead to distractions and negative opinions about the value of the experience.

Optimizing Short-Term Pair Relationships

When two people working together understand their Energies and Dynamics, the outcomes can be powerful. They are able to focus on tasks, manage handoffs and make the best use of what each of them brings to the situation.

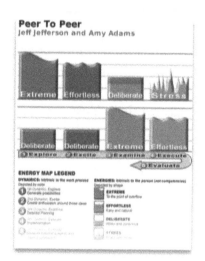

Peer To Peer
Jeff Jefferson and Amy Adams

5 Dynamics Peer-to-Peer reports focus on short-term relationships which are often more tactical in nature. An unlimited number and combination of Peer-to-Peer reports between yourself and other coworkers can be created through the 5 Dynamics application.

These reports are helpful in creating awareness between the two individuals so they can better prepare for their time together.

Optimizing Longer-Term Relationships for Growth and Influence

Partnerships where two people have a stake in each other's success and satisfaction benefit from a more in-depth look at how each of them can support the other's growth and development.

This may be in the form of a boss/subordinate relationship which incorporates management and performance conversations or more informal coaching and development. It may be in the form of relationships that influence one another where there is room for mutual learning and long term relationship building.

In either case, the 5 Dynamics Influence report provides more in-depth information how to best optimize this relationship.

An unlimited number and combination of Influence reports between yourself and other coworkers can be created through the 5 Dynamics application.

To facilitate the discussion between you and a coworker using either paired report, refer to the Conversation Guide worksheet below.

Pair Report Conversation Guide

Two people can best work out how to work together through a dialogue. **Having the *discussion* is even more important than the perceived accuracy of this report.**

	1. Explore	2. Excite	3. Examine	4. Execute
My Energies				
My Partner				
Energy	Asking "what-if"? Originating ideas. Trying to harmonize people, goals, objectives. Generating options.	Sees the world through "people." Outgoing, fun and optimistic. Enjoys creating enthusiasm for projects.	Serious. Sees things in black and white. Thinks much but speaks little. Precise. Critical and highly logical.	High need for action and closure. Competitive. Does everything quickly. Demanding and exacting.
	High need for **flexibility**		High need for **order**	
Dynamic	• Beginnings of projects. • Creating. • Innovating. • New strategies that connect disparate ideas.	• Raising enthusiasm. • Building teams. • Focusing on the "people" part of the job.	• Budgets. Data. Facts. • Creating logical plans. • Creating procedures. • Anticipating problems.	• Completing tasks. • Driving hard. • Holding people accountable.

CONVERSATION GUIDE
RECOMMENDED DISCUSSION QUESTIONS

FIRST: Write your intensities in each Energy, in row 2 on the preceding page. Add your colleague's in Row 3. Note the similarities and differences.

SECOND: Concentrate on the **greatest differences** first. How have those shown up in your working relationship when you both are in those Dynamics? How do you personally feel about spending a lot of time in those Dynamics where your Energy is lower? What does your counterpart think? How do you work together when you're in the Dynamic of a project where your intensities are similar?

THIRD: Think about the **value system** you bring to work. How does that show up in each Dynamic? Example: "I am very high in Execute. I value getting things done. I tend to have more respect for people like me, and less tolerance for those unlike me in that regard." How do such feelings serve you well? Serve you poorly? What does your counterpart think?

FOURTH: Look at the **highs and lows from left to right** in your Energies and Dynamics, from Explore to Evaluate. How does your interest/engagement naturally rise and fall at the beginning, middle, and end of any project? How does that affect your performance? What does your counterpart think? Have you seen any implications of this?

FIFTH: Consider aspects of **your past working relationship** that come to mind. Does this information suggest any explanations for the past behavior? *Based on what you're learned, what commitments can you make to improve the relationship in the future?*

Mike Sturm ended his communications with one word, "Namaste." Mike preferred this term as he believed that it summed up his life's work: "I recognize and honor the best in you and you recognize and honor the best in me." The legacy that Mike left behind was a methodology that shows you how to appreciate the best in yourself and how to value the best in others.

Summary

While it takes a conscious effort, engaging others in their own preferred learning style increases understanding and influence.

When two people understand each other's Energetic preferences, they are able to focus on tasks, manage handoffs and make the best use of what each of them brings to the situation.

In the next chapter, we will examine how 5 Dynamics can help optimize any team.

5. Getting It Done Together

{
"If you can determine what mixture of Energies a role or team needs and what mixture of Energies a person or team has, then you will create necessary conditions for success and satisfaction."

— Mike Sturm
}

Key takeaways

Understanding a team's Energies allows you to optimize the team's performance.

- Teams can experience predictable challenges due to their Energetic differences.
- 5 Dynamics can help to clarify these challenges, and can provide a neutral language for discussing them.

Imbalances of team Energy follow predictable patterns.

- An overlap of Energies may cause group-think.

- Differences in Energies may lead to tension and talking past each other.

Optimizing Team Performance

Teams are at their best when they can understand and align their Energies, so that they can work together with minimal wasted energy. The 5 Dynamics Team Graphs show all team members on one graph, reflecting the pattern of Energies across each Dynamic.

Teams can experience predictable challenges when the Energy in their Dynamics is out of balance.

5 Dynamics can help to clarify these challenges and can provide a neutral language for discussing them. It is clear where there are differences in intensity, revealing where there is either abundant or reduced Energy. This allows teams to understand their Energetic differences and incorporate that into designing internal work allocation or external work plans.

Research has shown that diverse teams have the potential for greater success, because of their broader repertoire of Energies to focus on the Dynamics of the process, which leads to client satisfaction.

It is important to remember that Energy does not equal competency, but it is the amount of Energy it takes someone to focus on that particular Dynamic. Do not make the mistake of allocating roles and responsibilities based on Energy only, as that will reduce developmental opportunities and potentially keep people "stuck" in their Effortless Energies.

Reading a Team Graph

Many people ask if there is a preferred amount of Energy in specific Dynamics on any given team that will predict success. Our response is, "Yes and No," since it depends on the task of the team as to which Dynamics are most important.

We recommend answering 5 key questions when looking at any team graph:

1. In which Dynamic(s) do you notice the most Energy?

This is usually an obvious area to find; however, notice that there may be more than one Dynamic with a high amount of Energy.

Also notice where the opposing Energy of this Dynamic is energetically.

Example: If there are three people on a team with high Energy in Explore and one person with high Energy in Examine, this is a flag to discuss how this potentially conflicting Energy shows up on the team.

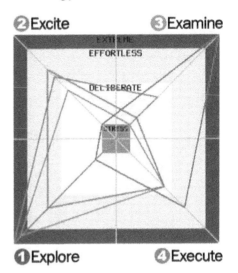

2. In which Dynamic(s) do you notice the least Energy?

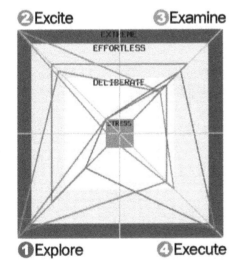

This may point to an area that is avoided by the team in general.

It could also point to individual struggle if one person is carrying all of the weight in any particular Dynamic.

Although people do prefer to perform in areas where their Energy is highest, it can take a toll on any one individual that has to continuously carry the team in a specific Dynamic.

Example: Having one person on the team that with high Energy in Execute while all other team members are lower could create a lot of work for the higher Execute Energy over time.

3. **In which Dynamic(s) do you see the biggest difference in Energy among members of the team?**

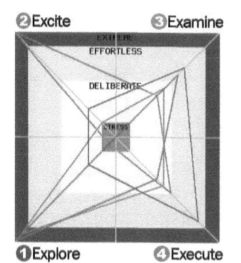

The purpose for answering this question is to get some insight on where there may be a lack of connection among teammates.

Example: If someone has Extreme Energy in Excite while another team member has Stress Energy in Excite, ask how these two communicate with each other in the team process.

Extreme differences in Energetic preferences can sometimes point to conflict if the group is not aware of each other's strengths. It's a great starting point for any team conflict.

4. **Who are the "connectors" among the team?**

These are people who may have higher Energy in Dynamics that directly following one another in the process cycle; these people can serve as a connector for others in those two Dynamics.

Example: Paul has Extreme Explore Energy but Deliberate Excite. Rachel has Stress Explore Energy but Extreme Excite. Todd has Effortless Energy in both Explore and Excite and serves as a connector for Paul and Rachel. These connectors can be crucial for moving an idea from start to finish.

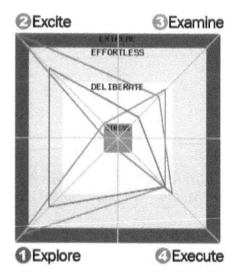

5. Who is the "Official" leader of the team?

Sometimes, the person responsible for team progress is not the one who shows up with the most directive Energy on the team.

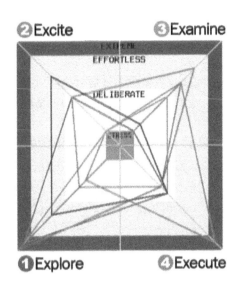

Example: Paul is the team leader and has Effortless Energy in Explore and Excite. Brian is not the team leader; however, he has Extreme Energy in Execute and shows up as a serious driver on the team.

Understanding this is useful and can help the official Team Leader determine how best to access the Energy of the team.

Tips for Talking about a Team Graph

- Starting at Explore, go around the cycle and discuss each Dynamic, having those members who have an Effortless or Extreme Energy intensity in that Dynamic describe what happens for them in that phase. Invite others to add what they notice about the descriptions of each Dynamic. Ask for specific examples and anecdotes as illustrations.

- Next, go around the cycle again and have members with Deliberate or Stress Energy intensity in each Dynamic describe how they approach that phase. Ask for specific examples and anecdotes as illustrations.

- Talk about where the team's Energies do and don't overlap.

- Discuss how to align your efforts by coordinating roles and tasks through Dynamics. If there is a striking imbalance of Energy, you may consider bringing in new team members or they can partner with other groups and individuals who are high in the dynamics in which they are low. 5 Dynamics provides the awareness, and with awareness comes choice.

Common Imbalances of Energy

Large differences of Energies may lead to differing approaches to a Dynamic, possibly resulting in tension and talking past each other.

Strong overlap of Energies may reduce the ability of the team to have different perspectives; group-think may dominate decisions.

Strong Dominance of Energy in a particular Dynamic

- A team with many members who have Effortless or Extreme Energy in the Explore Dynamic may be highly creative, but they may also spend an inordinate amount of time generating options, and may lack a sense of urgency.
- A team with high Energy in the Excite Dynamic may be good at engaging and motivating others, but they may also make impulsive decisions to keep harmony.
- A team with high Energy in the Examine Dynamic may be good at analyzing problems and developing plans, but they may lose sight of the big picture.
- A team with high Energy in the Execute Dynamic may be good at setting and achieving goals, but they may lack creativity and flexibility.

Consider Multiple Energy Patterns

A team's performance reflects how team members focus and align their Energies as they move through the process of learning, working and collaborating. There are multiple combinations of Energy patterns, and each one has unique ways of working, learning and collaborating.

Especially when a new team is launched or a new project started, taking time to identify the pattern created by the Energies of the team members can help anticipate areas that will need extra attention due to reduced Energy, and areas that will need to be watched for potential Energy overflow (as described above). Identifying these patterns ahead of time can reduce friction and help clarify expectations for performance.

The 5 Dynamics Learning Chart helps teams to identify their unique Energy DNA and how they match the Dynamics of the process. An unlimited number and combination of team Learning Charts can be created through the 5 Dynamics application.

Below are samples of some of the patterns you may experience; it is important to remember that there is a wide variation of patterns in any team.

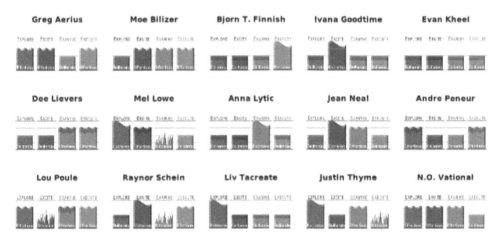

Summary

Using 5 Dynamics team tools, teams can understand and align their Energies, while avoiding predictable challenges in Energetic differences and designing winning strategies for any plan or project.

The 5 Dynamics Team Graph highlights overlaps and differences in Energies, allowing teams to actively identify and discuss potential pitfalls before they occur.

The 5 Dynamics Learning Chart helps teams match their Energies to the processes at hand and provides a shorthand for addressing each other's Learning preferences.

In Part III, we will look more closely at the applications of 5 Dynamics and how others are capitalizing on their investment in 5 Dynamics.

6. Practice Makes Perfect

{
"Success is the sum of small efforts—repeated day in and day out."

– Robert Collier
}

Key takeaways

5 Dynamics is grounded in a common process model which applies to all levels of your organization.

- This model is flexible enough to apply equally well to individuals, pairs, teams, enterprises or departments, and people outside your company.

- You can use this simple model to anticipate, explain, or interact with people at any level.

- The methodology provides a new way of looking at performance, increasing productivity by reducing process loss.

Beyond 5 Dynamics Fundamentals, we offer a series of Learning Labs designed to improve success and satisfaction across your entire organization.

By now you have learned how to use the 5 Dynamics Model to assist you in understanding your Energetic DNA, the Energetic DNA of others, and the Energetic DNA of teams. These are all valuable tools, but to build a culture of performance where innovation and engagement are released, you will need to assimilate the language and the methodology into your day-to-day work.

The beauty of 5 Dynamics is that it is like a Swiss army knife: one methodology can be integrated into multiple applications: Team Building, Conflict Resolution, Performance Development, Onboarding, Coaching, Mergers and Acquisitions, Leadership Effectiveness, Career Development, Project Management, etc. Basically any endeavor that requires human interaction can benefit from the 5 Dynamics Methodology.

To ensure that you maximize your investment in 5 Dynamics, we will share with you how our clients are capitalizing on their investment. Here is a little more information about the Core Model and the myriad of applications.

Core Model: The Success–Satisfaction Cycle

The five-phase Success and Satisfaction Cycle[SM] shows a sequence of how work, or other processes, move toward success and satisfaction. Your Energy intensities focus on each Dynamic so you can move through the Dynamics. Doing this in sequence creates outcomes that are innovative, engaging, well planned, and complete, as well as capturing knowledge to improve the process. Your Energy intensities provide the momentum to move around the cycle.

<u>A Common Model to Apply to Multiple Levels of Action</u>

Uniquely, the model underpinning 5 Dynamics relates individuals' and groups' Energies to the outside world, and to the process of getting things done. This model is flexible enough to apply equally well to individuals, pairs, teams, departments or enterprises, and people outside your company.

You can use this simple model to anticipate, explain, or interact with people at any level.

5 Dynamics: Adding Value at Every Level

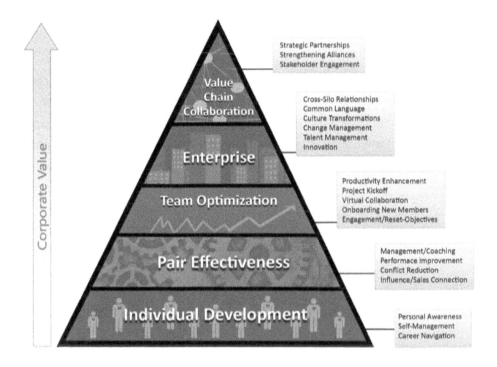

Increase Productivity by Reducing Process Loss

What happens when things break down is called *process loss*: steps were not completed; there were unclear expectations or poor communications between people moving through the process.

Everyone knows that the best-laid plans are ultimately vulnerable to personal relationships, office politics, and misperceptions. These "people problems" create internal friction which translates into process loss which is subtracted from actual productivity.

$$AP = PP - PL$$

Actual Productivity = People's Productivity – *Process Loss*

The 5 Dynamics methodology provides a new way of looking at performance. It combines a 5-step process model with an assessment of 4 individual Energies to provide an easy-to-apply method to focus on actions that will produce success and satisfaction.

What does Process Loss Look Like?

Individuals

You hired the best person for the role, yet they are not producing optimal results. People are stuck in an Energy and do not move effortlessly through the process. They do not understand how their natural Energies affect their perception and are not aware of their blind spots, which prevent them from making their optimal contribution.

Pairs

People are frustrated and blame others, they do not understand how others learn, work and collaborate, and they waste time talking past each other.

Teams

You put together this amazing team—but they are not collaborating well and spend too much time in meetings. They don't know how to focus each member on the work or how to support and inspire each other to create the greatest outcomes.

Enterprises

Groups don't value the work of other groups, they miss important handoffs and people seem frustrated and demotivated.

Value Chains

People "talk at" partners in the value chain, reducing innovation and market information.

How can 5 Dynamics Help?

It helps by providing the following:

- A **Model** for getting things done with more efficiency and engagement

- A **Framework** for optimizing individual and team performance

- A **Common Language** for building a culture of accountability and performance

- A set of **Online Tools** that show pair and team dynamics

Much like the 5 Dynamics assessment itself, the methodology is simple and it produces an extraordinary amount of information which can be applied quickly, easily, and painlessly—without judgement.

Summary

To build a culture of performance where innovation and engagement are released, you will need to assimilate the 5 Dynamics language and methodology into your day-to-day work.

The 5 Dynamics methodology can be integrated into any endeavor that requires human interaction and is flexible enough to apply equally well to individuals, pairs, teams, departments or enterprises, and people outside your company.

The 5 Dynamics methodology provides a new way of looking at performance to reduce process loss.

The final chapter will review the key points of the book and leave you with a simple way to focus your performance in any situation.

7. Conclusion

> "We do the best we can with what we know, and when we know better, we do better."
>
> —Maya Angelou

Our purpose in this book has been to introduce you to the 5 Dynamics methodology, its underpinnings, and its many benefits—for virtually every situation in your life (not just work). We've presented you with a basic framework for better understanding yourself, your dyad relationships, and your team relationships.

As with any talent, it takes time and practice to nurture these skills until they become second nature for you, but we think that you will find the effort well worth it for you and your colleagues.

As you put our methodology into practice, here are the core concepts to keep in mind:

Three Big Ideas that Drive 5 Dynamics

1. Our attention shifts as we move through the Dynamics of any process.
2. Our innate Energetic preferences drive our focus and our actions.
3. External *success* and internal *satisfaction* come from applying people's Energies to goals.

These three truths, summarized from Part I, form the underpinnings of the methodology and may be a good place to start when introducing 5 Dynamics to someone new.

Always Remember

With 5 Dynamics, the Energy intensity indicates the amount of effort, over time, which it will take to focus on a particular Dynamic.

- More intensity is not better!

- Energies are NOT competencies.

- Energies are NOT labels.

Particularly when applying 5 Dynamics to understanding others, it is tempting to dismiss them based on limited information about them (for example, "Our resident High Execute is on another rampage," or "Oh, you're low Examine; I'll find someone else to help me with this spreadsheet."), but those types of summary judgments are counterproductive.

As described in Part II, our relationships with others are key to finding success and satisfaction for ourselves. Mike's intention, partly, was to create a safe language to talk about our differences without the baggage of "personality." So keep these three reminders close at hand when dealing with others.

Four Questions for Focusing Performance

Finally, let us leave you with simple way focusing your performance at any point in a process. Just ask each other these four questions:

- What Energy am I in?

- What Energy are YOU in?

- What Dynamic are WE in?

- What Dynamic would produce the most success?

These questions will help keep you grounded in our methodology and, when used daily, can reduce the potential for conflict and process loss.

Namaste.

Appendix A: Case Studies

Case Study: Focus on *Team Development, Improving Working Relationships*

Nonprofit Health Care Organization

CHALLENGE

A nonprofit health care organization serving nearly 60,000 Alaska Native and American Indian people implemented an innovative method of providing primary care that is built around the needs of the patient and a team-based method of care delivery. Each Integrated Care Team (ICT) was made of a Provider, RN Case Manager, Administrative Support person and a Certified Medical Assistant. The organization realized that the ICT's ability to work interdependently was the key to success—that by building better relationships with each other and their patients, the quality of care would also improve.

The charge was twofold: 1) maximize the effectiveness of Integrated Care Teams and 2) teach a cadre of Providers and Nurses a strengths-based relational model of coaching so they could mentor both their teams and other ICT's.

The challenge was in meeting all the criteria: It had to teach teams in a method that was "easy to understand, practical and immediately applicable." Also, teams could not be out of clinic and away from patients for more than 90 minutes. Finally, the program had to support the organization's core competencies: Communication & Teamwork, Improvement & Innovation, Organization Care & Relationships, and Workforce Development Skills & Abilities.

ACTION

The organization chose 5 Dynamics to address these needs, and our methodology was included as a cornerstone of teaching teams to work together effectively. Each ICT member completed the 5 Dynamics Starting Point assessment, received a one-on-one debrief of his or her individual results, and then the team came together for a team debrief, with a focus on the team's collaboration styles and insights on strategies to support good teaming for their specific team makeup.

Within 93 minutes—3 minutes to complete the assessment and 90 minutes of training—teams began implementing the 5 Dynamics methodology.

Two pilot programs were developed and delivered to teach mentors a strengths-based relational coaching model. The first included clinical teams and administrative managers in the medical services division of the organization. The first pilot was so successful that a second pilot was expanded to also include non-clinical managers.

5 Dynamics played a feature role—the 5 Dynamics Performance Cycle was used to teach the coaching model; the mentors found it easy and intuitive to understand and apply. Having 5 Dynamics as the foundation for both team effectiveness and the coaching model had the added benefit of shortening the learning curve of the mentors significantly.

Feedback from the initial pilot programs was so positive that the organization decided that every ICT in the medical services division would complete 5 Dynamics and receive the individual and team debrief; now 5 Dynamics is a prerequisite for anyone working on a clinical team.

The results of the pilots also demonstrated that the model of coaching provided a practical, strengths-based methodology that is universally applicable; consequently, the coaching methodology is now being rolled out organization-wide to all leaders and others who 'coach' as part of their job (e.g. improvement advisors). In addition, 5 Dynamics is being integrated into other initiatives in which team collaboration is essential.

5 Dynamics has provided the ICTs with greater self-awareness and a better appreciation of differences in working styles; as a result, an immediate impact in teambuilding has been seen through increased trust and quality interpersonal interactions. Managers

RESULTS

are now learning to mentor their direct reports using a strengths-based model of development.

Ultimately, it is the patients who receive the greatest benefit: a high-functioning Integrated Care Team provides for better care and organization service.

By focusing on the organization, taking a systems approach, and providing easy-to-implement methodologies like 5 Dynamics, the organization was honored with the Malcolm Baldrige Award.

"A health care system owned and managed by Alaska's Native people has achieved astonishing results in improving the health of its enrollees while cutting the costs of treating them."

—The New York Times

"This is organizational vision and leadership at its very best...to achieve whole population health excellence for your organization-owners."

—Dave Ford, Former CEO, CareOregon

"I think it's the leading example of health care redesign in the nation, maybe the world."

—Don Berwick, Former Administrator, Centers for Medicare and Medicaid Services

Case Study: Focus on *Career development*

Industry-leading software company

CHALLENGE

Jason, a brilliant software architect at a very large software company, had been preparing for a promotion to the next level of management. He would be leading a team of 75 people. When he was passed over for the job, he stewed over the rejection for several months and put his resumé together.

ACTION

Having been selected for the company's high-potential leadership group, Jason attended a 5 Dynamics fundamentals program. While there, he had a crucial self-discovery: although he had rather high Energy in Excite (toward people) his entrepreneurial drive was much stronger. The 5 Dynamics report and the facilitator described this combination as "entrepreneurial."

RESULTS

Jason approached the 5 Dynamics facilitator during a break and told him, "I just called my boss and thanked him for not giving me that job. I realized I am really happy

doing what I do in my own little skunkworks: I develop ideas in Explore and can jump right to action in Execute. People and administrivia slow me down. I actually have a dream job doing what I am doing."

His highest Energies, Execute and Explore, told a simple story that lifted months of disappointment and bitterness.

Jason remains with the company and is going strong in his current job. In his online profile, the company refers to him as "Chief Architect and Visionary" in a major product area.

Case Study: Focus on *Organizational Roles, Performance Management*

Insurance Company

CHALLENGE

Contemplating the consolidation of many operations centers into just a few locations, a major insurance company was concerned about the risks of low retention and engagement during the eight-month process.

Potentially high attrition during the transition threatened the company's core back-office operations. A number of people were being moved to new roles and the Director of Leadership Development needed a unifying approach for re-engaging and focusing people on their work performance.

ACTION

5 Dynamics was chosen as a unifying framework because of its focus on work performance and not personality. Coaches used the Leadership Report in working with individuals to identify optimal roles in the new organization. Teams used the team tools to foster clearer understanding how to focus their energy on performance results. Managers used the individual reports to understand their employees, identify their strengths and coach them through the change process.

RESULTS

The strengths-based focus provided a refreshing view for employees to re-think where their talents could be best used in the new organization. The Director of Learning and Leadership Development reports, "It was easy to use at all levels and has had a major positive impact on engagement and retention."

Case Study: Focus on *Learning, Leadership Development*
Business School MBA Program

CHALLENGE

One of the Top 5 business schools in the U.S. needed to modify its pivotal first-year curriculum to meet the needs of an increasingly global student body. It wanted to accelerate the learning of new students and increase their self-awareness and understanding of their strengths as leaders and team members.

The Academic Director of the Executive Skills Program wanted to create greater individual leadership and team capability with the 450 first-year ("MBA1") MBA students. She wanted to update her curriculum with the latest tools and approaches. Students work in multiple teams, often on virtual teams. They needed a methodology and skills to reduce the start-up time when working on their 85 work-study projects to meet the expectations of their international corporate partners.

ACTION

After competitive review, 5 Dynamics was chosen as the foundational tool set to help the students understand their preferred leadership energies and strengths to mobilize performance at all phases of a learning process. All 450 MBA1 students received their individual reports and were coached by MBA2 coaches to understand how to focus their Energy on working, learning, and collaboration. The students used team graphs to accelerate the formation of their action learning teams, using the 5 Dynamics as the coaching model. As students join new teams during their two-year program, they will generate new team graphs each time to accelerate the team development process.

RESULTS

All 450 students have completed their 5 Dynamics assessment and received group orientation and individual coaching using the model. MBA2 coaches have rated the course 4.78 on a 5-point scale, a major improvement over prior years.

Case Study: Focus on *Effective Project Management*
Fortune 100 Company

CHALLENGE

One of our client companies was losing millions of dollars each year due to project restarts. The client held project kick offs and invited all of the relevant players. Oftentimes, the executive sponsors were too busy to attend. So, the project teams moved forward. The challenge came in when the executives decided to join a later meeting and would want to rethink the direction. This rework was costing the client millions of dollars.

ACTION

5 Dynamics worked with the company and taught them the 5 Dynamics language. We also shared the 5 Dynamics process model. We helped the executives to understand that they needed to join the meetings during the Explore phase of the project and not wait until the teams had moved into Examine or even worse Execute. The organization now uses 5 Dynamics flashcards to indicate what phase of the project they are on at any given time.

RESULTS

Just this simple change saved the company millions of dollars. It also provided a framework for running effective projects and it made it safe to discuss project stages.

Case Study: *Cultivating Your High Potentials*

Large Family-Owned Winery

CHALLENGE

An internationally renowned winery was attempting to amplify the outcomes of their annual High Potential Managers program, by which strategy was created using the combined knowledge of selected participants.

ACTION

At the end of a six month development program, the client tasked the High Potential Managers to present the executive leadership with specific recommendations to improve the company's growth.

The customer told us: "I designed this HiPo program to work as teams. I factored 5 Dynamics heavily throughout all of it. First they took the assessment to discover how they learn and work with others. I consciously formed the teams in such a way as to make sure all four Energies were represented, and I told them why. This made a huge difference—even more than I expected.

"I explained that everyone comes with unique gifts, skills, and energies. When you assemble a cohort team this way you get a balance of diverse styles. It creates higher-performing teams and accelerates their output.

"Together, these teams have developed innovative recommendations. It's been like action-learning where they would adjust styles and they use a balance of Energies, consciously, as their platform.

"They quickly gained consensus on their ideas. Before, at this point in the program teams were just scurrying about; that is now gone. They are cohesive, prepared, on track. They use the 5 Dynamics language in all their conversations as they move through the process of work.

RESULTS

"I have been doing high potential teams for 15 years. This was far and away the best, and the extensive use of 5 Dynamics was the only control factor I changed. They were much better prepared for their presentations, and they talk about how much they have learned from each other. They had a process. They worked through the 5 Dynamics, starting with Explore through Execute and Evaluate. It drove everything they did."

Case Study: Focus on *Teaming*

Compliance Legal Team at Financial Institution

CHALLENGE

A multi-national financial firm in a highly regulated environment depended heavily on its compliance team of 13 lawyers, and that team had become dysfunctional. The team lead "Barbara" called us because her group had splintered into a we/they mindset. Located four time zones apart, some teammates had stopped speaking and collaborating. She had made open communication a major emphasis and couldn't understand why her group wasn't improving. Barbara had heard from the company's executive team that 5 Dynamics could catalyze rapid changes in group performance and wanted to learn more.

ACTION

5 Dynamics developed a three-part strategy: measure / meet / follow up. First, the teammates anonymously completed our team assessment, measuring the group's view of its performance in terms of factors critical to their success. Lowest scores emerged in the areas of trust, external recognition, and leadership effectiveness.

The survey revealed a deeply skewed team, self-evaluating at opposite ends of the spectrum on many items. The highest was technical competence; the lowest three were trust, external recognition, and leadership effectiveness (also skewed toward extremes). In the composite of 5 Dynamics Energies, the team appears balanced, but just below the surface are two different factions comprising 10 people who have much different outlooks on the world. Barbara's inability to see "beyond her own Energies" contributed to her difficulty in knowing what was wrong and what to do about it.

A 5 Dynamics facilitator led a six-hour in-person modified Fundamentals session that taught the group about their Energies and how to apply them to work and to each other. Barbara learned how her own natural biases impeded her ability to understand and collaborate

ACTION

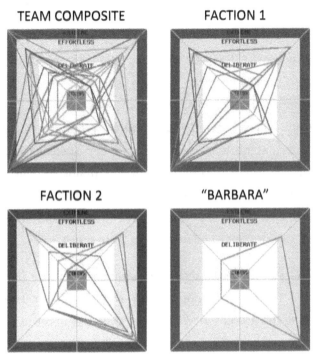

with her team. The team developed an effective, non-personal way of communicating about and sharing work. At the session they developed practical behavioral norms in the form of individual commitments.

One team member who had not spoken with Barbara in six months immediately asked to collaborate with her on mutual coaching. Barbara called the session "very constructive" and requested to continue working with 5 Dynamics to sustain the team's progress. The two "groups" now consider themselves one team, and collaborate productively together despite (or perhaps because of) their differences. 5 Dynamics was next invited to work in the general counsel's office.

It was fascinating to me, to become more aware of my work preferences (the assessment was spot-on), and it was interesting to see my colleagues in a new light. [The] enthusiasm and insights made it all very fun but also on a more serious note I am sure the discussions will help us start to communicate and work together more productively as a team.

— **Executive Director**

Appendix B: *5 Dynamics Foundations*

This is a reprint of an article written by Mike Sturm and Dr. Peter Nelson.

5 Dynamics Foundations of the Model and Assessment

Summary

- 5 Dynamics is a method, a way to work.
- Using this method, employees consider their work as a process.
- Each task in the process is best done with a particular type of concentrated focus, as well as a way of perceiving that task, and certain behaviors and ways of thinking that lead to easy, successful outcomes. We call each of these types of focus demanded by the work "Dynamics."
- Virtually all work can be described in five Dynamics: Explore, Excite, Examine, Execute, and Evaluate. For a given work processes these repeatedly appear in a sequence.
- Each individual naturally invests him or herself most naturally comfortably in certain Dynamics, and less easily in others. This differs from competence.
- "Energies" refer to people's natural ease in spending time and focus in each Dynamic. They refer to one's measured preferences for learning, perceiving, collaborating, and behaviorally working. These Energies correspond to the first four Dynamics: Explore, Excite, Examine, Execute.
- Before using the 5 Dynamics method, individuals measure their own Energies through a rigorous psychometric assessment that is delivered online.
- They then use the work-based process model to apply their own, and other people's energies, to achieve the optimal external business results ("Success") and their highest internal engagement ("Satisfaction").

This paper provides you with background into the method—an adaptation of the Gestalt Cycle of Experience—and the development of the Assessment, which measures how people prefer to engage in that Cycle.

The 5 Dynamics Model

- Process models now dominate the business landscape.
- Knowledge industries apply process tools.
- No process tools adequately measure and incorporate the human element.
- Much of these companies' asset values, and upsides and vulnerabilities, reside in human factors.
- 5 Dynamics addresses this opportunity.

The 5 Dynamics method and model are based around work process. We have designed them to equip people with the tools they need to get work done. Benchmarks of effectiveness include greater externally measured success, and higher internal satisfaction or engagement for employees.

The past few decades have seen the emergence of a variety of work process-based models, including Six Sigma, Lean, TQM, BPM, BPR, QMF, and others. Although many originated in manufacturing environments, information technology has created a larger Knowledge Economy, and so they now are extensively applied in enterprises that produce no physical goods (as well as those that still manufacture). The intrinsic value of such a company is locked up not only in its patents, but also in the intellectual capital of its employees, their internal and external relationships, and their ability to innovate, collaborate, and execute.

Unfortunately, there is no rigorous way to capture that value on a balance sheet, so it is usually ignored. What gets measured gets done. What can't get measured gets overlooked. Also, when actually implemented, most of the process approaches mentioned above tend to diminish the criticality of the "human element". They may pay attention to information flows and competencies, but every executive knows that the best laid plans are ultimately vulnerable to the vagaries of personal relationships, office politics, agendas, misperceptions and misunderstandings, job mismatches, time sinks from "people problems", internal friction, uncontrollable relationships with stakeholders, the quality of LOB distributed leadership, and the like.

This is precisely the gap that 5 Dynamics fills. It is the only approach that maps the people to the process. When that correspondence is clear, understood, and shared, people can move forward rapidly.

Our model of process is designed to be simple, flexible, and universal. Any user can map his workflow to it, and find that the mapping varies very little over time. Because of the simplicity (five descriptive terms to be discussed shortly) it can become a common language for an enterprise. People can objectively discuss work, and their contributions, in unambiguous terms that carry no emotional baggage.

The 5 Dynamics Differentiator

Mapping People to Process

- 5 Dynamics has its origins in Gestalt Psychology and process thinking.
- Subjective perception catalyzes the way we understand the world and how we get things done.
- 5 Dynamics draws from Gestalt's orientation toward perception, action, energy and goal completion.
- This is a process, and it explains many of the business results that companies achieve.

The 5 Dynamics model stems from the work its founder Michael Sturm did as a Gestalt psychologist. Gestalt concerns the ways in which people organize their relationships with their environments, and move through a cycle of concentrated focus and application of their energy to achieve their goals. Edwin and Sonia Nevis at the Gestalt Institute in Cleveland certified Sturm.

Gestalt looks at how people become aware of certain stimuli in the world, which stimuli they "select" to act upon, the energy they invest in that action, where they get stuck, and how that interaction changes (or doesn't alter) subsequent interaction with another similar stimulus.

To apply this model to the corporate world: a CEO may announce five new programs at a strategy offsite. Attendees make sense of the totality differently. Their focus gravitates toward some, and not others. They make meaning based on what they already have known or experienced, even though the CEO wants them to "innovate". Having made sense of it, they decide how much energy to invest in which initiatives. Next, their energy rises and falls according to predictable patterns as they work through the subtasks. As the goal is accomplished, their energy and focus diminish, and they become available to the next stimulus and focus. This goes on constantly, in a fractal fashion, in everything we do.

Sturm felt this model was too complex and abstract. He wanted to empower workers (he calls them "co-learners") to recognize where their natural energies would most comfortably take them, and enable them to use this knowledge and navigate the world successfully, and with the least stress. Individuals begin to align their strengths with the needs at hand, and rely on others (and offer support) where tasks that demand more energy might slow them down.

Sturm noticed that accomplishing many tasks in a process required people to pass through five phases (or Dynamics) that often appeared in this approximate sequence:

- First Dynamic: Understand the complete situation, see relationships, and develop creative solutions.

- Second Dynamic: Invest your energy exciting other people about the idea. Bust silos and develop internal support. Build a team.

- Third Dynamic: Develop an implementation plan using data. Create schedules, budgets, timetables, clear roles and rules, etc. Predict problems. Find faults.

- Fourth Dynamic: Aggressively implement the plan. Hold people accountable. Measure performance. Compete. Strive for completion.

- Fifth Dynamic: Assess the preceding four Dynamics with a two-pronged test: external success (e.g., cost, time, quality, profit) and internal satisfaction (engagement, absence of stress). Adapt the process to increase success and satisfaction in the next cycle.

A Gestalt Example: Your Latest Mission-Critical Initiative

		Your Company's Slogan Here

One Face or Two?

You call an all-hands meeting and announce a critical new initiative. How does your audience understand these sound waves and visual images you transmit?

Bombarded with stimuli, people perceive the world very selectively. We see "what we want to see," but the 'wanting' is actually not entirely conscious. It tends to fit prior patterns and relationships, what "makes sense."

Do you see a white triangle floating atop a black triangle overlaying three circles?

No triangles or circles exist, floating or otherwise. There are just lines and shapes. To survive, early man learned to make sense of shapes, signs, forms, and edges, and apply them to what he had seen before. Is that a lion in the grass?

How do employees make sense of, and then act, on the command: "You've got to change the way you do business!"?

Enterprises constantly announce new initiatives and hope for "alignment" and buy-in. But employees selectively perceive the announcement, process the information differently, evaluate what it implies for them, and take action with varying degrees of intensity, focus, and purpose.

Gestalt psychology follows that long trail from perception to action (or inaction) in the outside world. It asks three questions:
- What do you see?
- How do you understand it?
- What do you do with it?

We also ask, "Where in that process might you lose your focus?"

The Point: 5 Dynamics looks at people's preferred ways of understanding the world, and how they want to move" or take action around those perceptions. This is their "process." Is it optimal for the need?

If an individual, pair, or team heeded the Dynamics, completed them in the right order, didn't overdo or ignore any, and took the time to reflect on process improvements at the end, they would become more externally successful. This would appear as revenue, profit, cost reduction, quality, innovation, customer satisfaction, cycle time, or any other quantifiable business metric.

This was not the whole picture, however. He also found that success depended on employees' satisfaction with the work, and with their colleagues.

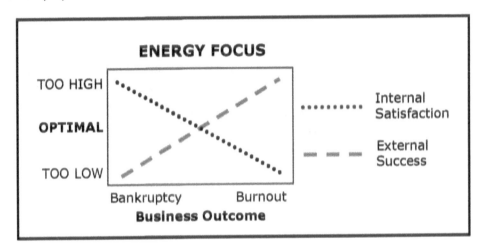

We have found this model to be universally applicable to jobs, roles, or larger processes that businesses conduct. With a small amount of training, employees can automatically understand what Dynamic the work ought to be in and actually is in. The next step is for the person to understand what Energies he has, and how they align with the current work Dynamic. For that, Sturm spent many years developing the 5 Dynamics assessment.

The 5 Dynamics Assessment
- The dimensions of the assessment directly match the first four Dynamics.
- The brevity of the assessment is an essential design feature. It took almost 10 years of continuous work to develop it.
- The assessment simultaneously measures individuals' preferences for learning, collaborating, and important aspects of behavior in task environments.

- The assessment does not measure competence, and does not use personality theory.
- It began as a learning style assessment. Its foundations are in cognitive and behavioral theory.
- It has been rigorously researched tested. Reliability can vary, however, with the person's overall mental state.
- The assessment's validity and reliability are very high. Statistical metrics are available in a separate white paper.

During the 1960s, much of the psychometric community was preoccupied with studies of the authoritarian personality. This was of course a very popular topic at the time, due to World War II and the Cold War. While studies like Milgram's shock experiment and Zimbardo's mock prison received great publicity, many other lesser-publicized academics were pursuing research on their own. W. Michael Sturm, 5 Dynamics' founder, attended American International College where he began experiments into authoritarian personality types.

His advisor at that time was Dr. Richard Sprinthall, (who subsequently wrote the critically acclaimed textbook on statistical methods for psychometrics) who, like Sturm, was interested in psychometrics and the authoritarian personality. In doing this research, Sturm looked at two specific tools about the authoritarian personality: the F-test of T.W. Adorno and the Dogmatism Test by Milton Rokeach. This early work culminated in a lead article in the Journal of Social Psychology.

Those two instruments familiarized him with scalar approaches to belief systems. At the same time he was working on the Locus of Control assessment of Julian Rotter, which measured the degree to which people believe the origin of behavioral reinforcement is internally or externally generated. Rotter also heavily influenced clinical psychology with the thesis that personality is the interaction of the individual's drives with the environment, and thus was context-sensitive rather than absolute. Sturm also worked extensively with two of the major learning-style assessments, the Wechsler Adult Intelligence Scale (WAIS), which measured verbal and performance IQs, and the Wechsler Intelligence Scale for

Children (WISC). The combination of studies provided a new understanding of the dogmatism F-test as well as grounding in learning theory.

Sturm was able to look at testing in an unusual way because he approached it as a social psychologist rather than as a clinical counseling psychologist. The difference is critical: Clinical psychologists test X to measure X. Social psychologists put people in situations where they think they are doing X, but they are really doing Y. Moreover, to Sturm the ultimate score isn't nearly as important as watching the process of the person undertaking the experiment.

Consistent with the principles of social psychology, the process through which people work becomes more important than the ultimate result. The majority of people's lives are not spent in outcomes, but in the journey toward achieving them. Observations of these journeys, or processes, therefore yield much more information than ultimate outcomes or scores. In part as a consequence of this belief, 5 Dynamics' tools are process-based: they examine how a person works, not just what his or her ultimate output might be.

This practice subsequently became useful in the development of the 5 Dynamics assessment; by watching thousands of people take assessments, he observed that most people's attention broke between the 24th and 28th items. It became a long-term goal, therefore, to reduce the number of items in any test to 24 or fewer.

The experience also afforded a perspective of process long before the notion of process was considered important. Sturm pursued his doctoral thesis at the University of Missouri under Dr. Charles Krauskopf who had been working on a test called the Personality Assessment System (PAS) that stemmed from the research of John Gittinger and David Saunders.

The PAS studies the relationship between intelligence and other personality variables as they interact to influence human behavior. It was closely related to the WAIS or the WISCR, albeit translated into a statistical analysis that enabled a psychologist to determine where a person would appear on scales—such as regulated or flexible, internal or external, a la Rotter, or role-adaptive or unadaptive. The PAS also included the concept of energy and it was contextually predictive. It enables the prediction of human behavior. Ultimately this test was extensively used by the CIA and Fortune 500 executives for high-level staffing.

There were many correlations between the PAS and the Wechsler tests, so Sturm set the goal of bringing some of the PAS concepts back to learning, which had been a lifelong passion. He began observing the patterns of test takers when he administered instruments such as the Ravens Progressive Matrices (a visual test), or the WISC-R or the WAIS, or the Slossen Verbal/Oral Test, or a spelling/writing example. He methodically mapped out the process that the student applied to complete the test. Over a period of time he began to see patterns in these behaviors as well as correlations between the patterns and the test outcomes. However, the process often delivered more information than the test score. For example, children approach tasks in a particular way based not on what they have learned, but on how they naturally go about doing things. He also observed the same phenomenon with adults

Sturm began fashioning his own test instrument with a set of polarities different from those of Gittinger and Saunders. These had to do with learning, but also with focus and energy.

PAS	5 DYNAMICS
Externalizer/Internalizer	Focuses on Details/Focuses on Whole
Rigid/Flexible	Verbal/Visual and Touch
Acceptable/Unacceptable	Logical/Intuitive
	Factual/Imaginative
	Sequential/Associative
	Relates rationally/Relates empathetically
	Time-oriented/Space-oriented
	Thinking-oriented/Action-oriented

These disparate scales, however, considered severally do not tell a coherent story. Sturm also was able to deduce patterns, or clusters of scores that fit meaningfully large subgroups. These clusters are quite important, because they enable an assessment to make deductive inferences.

In common language, the terms left-brained and right-brained describe certain combinations of traits or patterns. In point of fact, only 67 percent of "right-brain-dominant" people are left-handed. The traits associated with one hemisphere might also be located in the other hemisphere, as a product of genetics and hormonal activity. Moreover, many brain functions are so complex as to be carried out in both hemispheres, sometimes serially and sometimes in parallel. The terms "left-brain dominant" and "right-brain dominant" are able to convey meaning, even though their literal physiological underpinnings may be suspect. Sturm was able to identify similar patterns and overlay them on a series of polarities and an understandable sequence—producing a simplified version of the Gestalt Cycle of Experience.

By this time Sturm had become a differential diagnostician for learning differences. The prevailing belief at this time was that children who performed poorly in school were either brain damaged or learning disabled. Sturm again took a contrarian view: they were learning-different and likely brain-different. He found that if he understood a child's learning process, and matched it to a teacher with a similar process, and also helped the parents adapt to the process, the results were remarkably successful. The theory culminated when he became director of Special Education for three school districts in the State of Maine, and in three years raised the reading levels of the special education students by 3.5 years.

He observed how children would actively engage in certain types of learning activities and then would pull back from other parts of the process. That engagement he termed "energy" and the energetic shift determined more about a student's success than did anything else in the process.

At this point Sturm spent three years with at the Gestalt Institute of Cleveland under the direction of Edwin Nevis. Gestalt psychology is both process- and energetically-based, and so there was a natural concordance between Sturm's prior work and that of the Gestalt Institute's. At that time, the concept of resistance held much sway in Gestalt circles. Sturm did not accord nearly as much weight to resistance (His view since has become mainstream.) and rather saw resistance as a neurological phenomenon. As he saw it, people didn't expend energy to stop something. Rather, they did not have the energy to complete something. That requisite energy was invested elsewhere. This also conflicted with some of the pathological basis of Gestalt theory in those years. Sturm viewed people's fundamental processes as open to improvement, but not wholesale change. "Resistance", for example, was usually an outcome of selective perception and inadequate energy to move through the Cycle, as opposed to neurosis or psychosis.

Upon graduating from the Gestalt Institute in 1983, he began working in earnest on the assessment that is in use today. He became grounded in L.L. Thurston's theory of "just noticeable differences." This is a statistical technique for measuring how people make decisions along a continuous spectrum when the differences between items can be very small. It applies to physical phenomena such as weights of objects, as well as to attitudes and opinions. The choice they make is almost invariably right, but when the items are close together, they choose in an unconscious fashion.

In light of Sturm's prior experiences as a social psychologist, this was a fitting statistical approach. At the point of just noticeable differences, a person cannot really think about, verbalize or be aware of what he or she really is doing. This understanding goes far to assure a more valid result.

The word choices on the assessment Sturm developed were the product of countless hours of experimentation. In selecting the words, Sturm presented thousands of words to people, asking them to rate the reaction they caused on a seven-point Likert scale.

By continuously paring out the terms that fell between the two tails, he was able to reduce the population of words. Meanwhile, through observation, assessment, third-party evaluations and interviews, he was able to correlate the selection of words to the Energy, preferences and learning styles of his test-taking population. As this was done without the availability of personal computers, the process was extremely laborious.

Consecutive iterations of the assessment reduced the number of items from 1200 to 120 to 72 to 36 to 24 to 18. With each successive reduction, the measurements of validity and reliability actually rose.

In a sense, the test is neither rationally assembled nor rationally completed. It is based on elicited response of emotions provoked by specific terms. This is not a cognitive form of self-examination. At the same time, people do not behave in a cognitive way because fundamentally they are not rational. People complete the assessment by making neurophysiologic "choices," below their cognitive level.

Neurophysiological Assumptions

- The principles of synaptic efficiency and pruning underpin explain some of the assessment's validity and reliability.
- People make the word-choices unconsciously and emotionally, and are subsequently justified by the more rational parts of the brain.

The brain comprises only 4% of body mass but consumes 20% or more of blood glucose, the compound that the body converts to create muscular and mental activity. In this sense, the brain is inherently inefficient, and thus it seeks to conserve energy through the principle of synaptic efficiency; it has been demonstrated that the brain tends to route neural messages along the most efficient (electrically least resistive) pathways. Applying this principle to the 5 Dynamics assessment, we see that the socially oriented person will "see" the socially oriented word foremost; this occurs because the neural pathways of the brain that control social function are the most efficient. Thus, the brain selects the socially oriented word and sends it to the parts of the brain that understand socialization. These connections have been corroborated by cross-validating 5 Dynamics' instruments with other independent assessments. (See the Validity & Reliability Summary.)

Unlike some traditional assessment tools that attempt to label and measure aptitude, competencies, or personality features, 5 Dynamics' assessment is architected on a radically different model. In terms of current understandings of brain function, the working hypothesis is that when presented with a computer-based assessment containing a selection of words, the brain registers all of the words, but only one of them may, for example, correspond most closely to a person's preferred way of doing things. The brain is a top-down processor that seeks to recognize what it already knows. Life experiences and positive reinforcement lead to the formation of neural networks that react to the presentation of particular stimulus patterns. Limbic-frontal connections in the brain provide positive emotional valence for a preferred stimulus resulting in an "Ah-ha experience" as described in the Gestalt theory of perception.

Thus the subject perceives the socially oriented word as most charged with energy and activates the neural networks for a positive response to socialization. In a broader sense, it is hypothesized that the destinations of these messages control the individual's preferred modalities of perceiving, learning, doing and collaborating. Discrimination and decision-making are pre-frontal brain functions, but these activities are always colored by the energetic charge that the limbic (emotional) brain provides through direct connections of the limbic system to frontal areas. In order to cut through the noise of additional words presented by Thurston pairs, the input pathways probably activate limbic pathways to a critical threshold and, hence, achieve an emotional charge that leads to the selection of one word out of the four.

This is not a conscious process although the mind subsequently rationalizes the choice by applying reason or logic to it through post-hoc attributions of value and meaning.

(Secondary neural value-laden and overly cognitive consideration is to some degree responsible for the assessment's validity in light of its relative brevity. In addition, the Internet-delivered assessment measures the latency between choices. The longer the latency, the more conflicted the test-taker is, i.e., there may be conflicting outcomes from several competing neural networks. This can be filtered recursively back into the scoring algorithm. Likewise, a rapid choice suggests a strong discriminatory process and a clear preference for one modality over others. Or, again, there are fewer conflicting networks and the dominant network requires less time to assert itself as the choice-maker.)

About the Authors

Michael Sturm, Founder. Mike's professional training included the fields of social, counseling, Gestalt, learning and educational psychology. Mike had a M.A. in Psychology and worked on his Ph.D. in Psychology at the University of Missouri. He had over 20 years of experience in education, serving in roles as a Teacher, Principal, Differential Learning Diagnostician, Director of Services for Exceptional Children and Director of Creative Learning at the elementary, junior/senior high and adult levels. He taught in, directed or founded schools/programs in traditional, British Primary, open classroom or creative learning and arts. He began working with assessments in the early 1960's focusing on communications and learning.

Dr. Peter L. Nelson, Research Director. Peter is a psychologist and social scientist with a deep background in statistics and neurobiology. His work began with psycho-physiological studies of the human brain with particular regard to the processes of consciousness, arousal and perception. This interest led to participation in research projects in neuroscience in the United States, England and Denmark. By the early 1980s, Dr. Nelson had become a social scientist focusing his research on how people experience and understand reality— whether seen through the visions of mystics or the daily perceptions of businessmen and businesswomen. Since then, he has worked for governments, nonprofits and businesses as a research consultant on projects ranging from end-user ethnography and U.S. national surveys to usability research and corporate cultural analysis. He is the author of numerous refereed articles in professional journals, as well as several books.

Appendix C: *Validity & Reliability*

This is a reprint of a white paper published by 5 Dynamics.

Validity & Reliability of the 5 Dynamics Assessment

<u>Background</u>

Face Validity

W. Michael Sturm, founder of 5 Dynamics, created the assessment over a 25-year period of research and development. The assessment uses the method of paired comparisons, a widely accepted and well-researched psychological assessment technique. The assessment was initially developed empirically to match learning and teaching styles in the school environments. The assessment has been continually refined and improved over the past twenty-eight years to produce the current Internet-delivered version. In our experience with client self-reporting, the assessment and its results have shown over 90% validity and reliability as determined by the more than 60,000 administered clients in business, industry, and educational applications.

Substantive/Structural Validity

The assessment is based on a combination of Paired Comparisons and Task Completion rendered through a model based on the Gestalt energy/cycle-completion framework. The methods of paired comparisons are based on Thurstone's Law of Comparative Judgment. L.L. Thurstone was the first to apply statistical analysis to psychological testing. When a person is presented with a stimulus, such as a word-pair or a picture, a sequence of events occurs. First the distal stimuli are patterned on the retina, then transferred into electrical signals and delivered to the brain. The brain then sets up mental representations using separate groups of neurons, one group for each stimulus. A complex psycho-physiological transformation then occurs, which triggers a series of electrochemical events in the cells of the brain. In the case of the 5 Dynamics assessment, when an individual is presented with word pairs for comparison, a neurological mechanism triggers two mental representations—one for each of the word pairs. The representation that the individual more prefers will create the higher neurological signal strength, causing that pair to be selected. Although an individual believes that they are consciously "choosing" one of the word pairs, in reality, it is the electrochemical process within the brain that applies certain rules and controls the response in a somewhat reflexive manner. Thurstone's method of "paired comparisons" is psychologically measurable and a possible mathematical description of the mechanism is described in a paper, "Probabilistic Psychophysics with Noisy Stimuli," by Ennis and Mullen, published in *Mathematical Social Sciences, 23*, (1992).

Development of the assessment started in 1983 and there have been three previous versions comprised, respectively, of 120 comparisons, 72 comparisons and 30 comparisons.

The original versions were designated as the Brainstreaming Inventory. The "pencil and paper" assessment versions were administered to over 15,000 subjects from the 1980s through the middle 1990s. The current 5 Dynamics assessment is a randomized online software implementation based on the most current 18+ word-pair comparison.

Research and development began by using a 7-category Likert scale, valued 1-7, to weigh over 600 words for their polarity. Words were given to a sample of educators, adults from many occupations and college students. Previously, the individuals from this sample had taken a battery of standardized tests that categorized them as people whose brain processes were generally more "left hemispheric" or "right hemispheric"; more "internal" or "external"; "concrete" or "abstract"; more "rigid" or flexible"; more "logical" or "intuitive"; and more "personal" or "impersonal" in their processing styles. Once the words were weighted using Likert methods and statistics were analyzed, the more positively weighted words were placed into paired comparisons. The samples were tested and retested at least four more times over eighteen months using the word-pair comparisons, Thurstone methods and statistical analysis. The paired comparisons and weights became part of the assessment in subsequent forms.

The assessment uses four domain variables representing four of the five processes of 5 Dynamics' Success/Satisfaction Cycle: Explore, Excite, Examine, and Execute. These process domain variables are categorized by their intensity strengths from a maximum of Extreme down to a minimum of Stress. For the purposes of this document we will use the designators, S, M, A, C. The S, M, A, C designators are mapped in this manner: Explore = S, Excite = M, Examine = A, Execute = C.

Validity and Reliability

Temporal Reliability/Form Equivalence

Individual 5 Dynamics assessment tests are constructed at the time they are requested using randomly selected word-pair comparisons. The word-pair comparisons are selected from a database of specifically classified word-pairs representing process phases of the Success/Satisfaction Cycle.

Since the 5 Dynamics assessment measures process variables dispersed categorically at the specific point in time that it is administered, temporal reliability is not primary to demonstrating the external validity of this assessment. Nevertheless, as seen below, test-retest reliability is very high. A subject may change slightly over time depending on their current situation and circumstances and the amount of time they have been exposed to the specific situation and circumstances. For example, if a subject who is low in the "Execute Energy" is forced to manage a large complex project, their "Execute Energy" score may rise a little.

Summarized results of studies conducted in the 1990s with various clients are presented in Table 1 on the next page. The six (6) reliability studies used the statistical method of Pearson Product Moment Correlation Coefficient and a post two-tail t-test to measure the reliability and degrees of freedom variance. These results are all statistically significant at the .05 level and not patterned with lower reliability coefficients as would be expected with subjects who might show slight increases depending on life circumstances. The consistently high reliability demonstrated a decline as the sampling went from adults to college students to high school students.

Table 1: Reliability scores for test-retest of all four phases—S, M, A, C

Organization	Test-Retest Time	N	S†	M†	A†	C†
Seagate Software & Kinkos; Orlando, FL	2 days	248	0.91*	0.88*	0.93*	0.90*
University of Maine; Augusta	9 Weeks	121	0.85*	0.78*	0.87*	0.86*
Security Plastics, Inc; Miami Lakes, FL; San Juan, Puerto Rico; & McAllen, TX	4 Weeks	376	0.81*	0.82*	0.94*	0.91*
Growth Associates International, Inc.; Boston, MA; Portland, ME; Boca Raton, FL; & Albany, NY	7 days	456	0.85*	0.87*	0.86*	0.82*
Sample of College Students	~9 months	427	0.79*	0.73*	0.83*	0.84*
Sample of High School Students (grades 10-12)	~8 months	268	0.71	0.72	0.76	0.75

†Values for S (Explore), M (Excite), A (Examine), and C (Execute) are Pearson Product Moment Correlation scores.

*t-test for significance of the correlation coefficient being greater than zero is $p \leq 0.05$

Most of the above reliability studies and the validity studies given below were conducted on behalf of the University of Maine and the State Department of Maine. Every teacher and administrator participant earned three re-certification credits to be counted towards their professional accreditation. These courses' three credits were studied and approved by the research and teaching committees of the University of Maine and by the State of Maine's Commissioner of Education after rigorously applied research into the courses' content, assessment tools and teaching/learning process methods. Also, the assessment tool was used in several school districts by their superintendents after they, their school board members and their school management teams were trained.

Internal Consistency

Reliability is a necessary condition but it is not a sufficient condition for validity. The additional conditions for validity are presented below.

Construct/Content Validity

The development process for the above mentioned set of word-pairs began over 25 years ago. The word-pairs were developed, chosen and subgroups were weighted using the following methodology:

In the 1980s, six different studies were conducted by clients with educational psychologist and 5 Dynamics founder W. Michael Sturm. Each study had between 150 and 300 subjects.

1. Word-pairs were chosen using a seven category Likert scale methodology. Only word-pairs that scored 7 (complete agreement, maximum score) on the Likert scale in all prior testing of subjects were chosen.

2. The word-pairs in (1) were presented as comparisons to a known sample group of only Extreme (no Stress) and only Stress (no Extreme) in the four variables. Pearson Product Moment Correlations were calculated for these groups and the category 7 word-pairs. A significant positive correlation was found with the Extreme sample groups and a significant negative correlation with the Stress sample groups ($p \leq 0.05$).

3. Overall Likert scaling was used to select the 72 word-pairs and weights that, until recently, comprised the assessment word-pair database.

4. Subsequently, the word-pair database was reduced from 72 pairs to 56 pairs. This reduction was based on two years of data gathered from the 72 word-pair assessment outcomes. Statistical averaging and percentile frequency was done on every word-pair within specified energy intensities (Extreme, Effortless and

Deliberate) of all four of the Success/Satisfaction Cycle's (S/SC) phases: Explore (S), Excite (M), Examine (A) and Execute (C). Only 14 word-pairs from the highest percentile frequencies within each phase were selected. This refinement from 72 selected word-pairs to 56 selected word-pairs was statistically analyzed for its efficacy in 2006.

External Validity

In the studies summarized in Table 2, subjects were given the 5 Dynamics assessment instrument and then they were asked to complete a self-rating (Likert method: 1-7) of the short versions of the "assessment" phase descriptors as applied to themselves or workshop colleagues. Statistical analysis was applied to the two highest phase scores and descriptor ratings in each study.

Table 2: Validity measures of 5 Dynamics assessment made against self-rating

Organization	Participants	N	Highest Phase Correlation†
Maine State Department of Education; Augusta, ME	Educators	210	0.87*
Growth Associates workshop; Boston, MA	Lay Adults	67	0.84*
Workshops for the Maine State Department of Education; Augusta, ME	Educators	487	0 .92*
Security Plastics, Inc.; Miami Lakes, FL; San Juan, Puerto Rico; McAllen, TX	Employees	376	0.85*
University of Maine; Portland, ME	Faculty & Students	214	0.82*
University of Maine; Presque Isle, ME	Workshop Attendees	86	0. 91*
University of Maine; Augusta, ME	Re-certification Workshop Attendees	203	0.87*

†Comparisons made between highest 5 Dynamics assessment 'Phase' and either self-ratings of the participants or ratings made by colleagues attending the workshop sessions. *t-test for significance of the correlation coefficient being greater than zero is $p \leq 0.05$.

In other studies, 5 Dynamics assessment results were compared to other external measures that test related constructs. In all of the studies summarized in Table 3 below, the statistical analyses applied were the Pearson Product Moment Correlation. Significance was set at p = 0.05.

Table 3: Validity measures of 5 Dynamics assessment made against other related measures

Organization	Participants	N	5 Dynamics Measures	Other Measures	Pearson Correlations
Growth Associates; Boston, MA	Lay Adults	67	"I-E" scores	Julian Rotter's Internal-External Test	0.82*
Growth Associates; Boston, MA	Lay Adults	67	"Left-Right" process scores	Rokeach's Open and Closed Mind Test	0.84*
Growth Associates; Boston, MA	Lay Adults	19	Related 5 Dynamics Assessment Sections	Personality Assessment System of Gittinger and Saunders (PAS)	I-E = 0.79* RA-RU = 0.85* R-F = 0.83*
University of Maine; Presque Isle, ME	Educators	74	"Left-Right" process scores	Raven Progressive Matrices	0.74*
University of Maine; Augusta, ME	Educators	146	5 Dynamics Profile	Loye's HCP (Hemispheric Prediction Grid) Profile Test	0.92*
American Cancer Society; Boston, MA	Lay Adults	42	5 Dynamics Profile	Left-Brain and Right-Brain descriptors	0.88*
American Cancer Society; Boston, MA	Lay Adults	56	5 Dynamics Hemispheric Preference Scores	Miller's "BrainStyle Inventory"	0.86*

*t-test for significance of the correlation coefficient being greater than zero is p ≤ 0.05.

Conclusion Validity

Different groups of individuals were taught using the assessment and not using the assessment. Results of the learning were measured and statistically compared to see if the assessment groups' learning was significantly improved in comparison to control groups (non-Assessment groups). In addition, members of teams and work performance were also studied in relation to the use of the assessment results.

The statistical method used in all of the studies summarized below is the "t-test." A probability ≤ 0.05 was set as the level of significance and was achieved in each study.

The samples, types of comparisons-predictions, and validity scores were as follows:

1. At the University of Maine in Fort Kent and Presque Isle, a total of 86 educators in different training programs with a minimum of twelve trainees in each group took the assessment tool and were taught using the Success/Satisfaction Cycle's (S/SC) phases for individual class instruction and for teaming the participants. These educators were compared to two control groups (twenty-nine educator members) where the instructor did not give the assessment nor teach the classes using the Cycle's methods. Each group was pre-tested for content knowledge and post-tested for the same content using identical questions and scoring. The difference in the individuals' test scores were the measurements used to compare the results of the experiment's two groups. The result is as follows:

$t = 2.89$, $p ≤ 0.05$ (significant difference)

2. For Growth Associates, Boston, MA, 19 six-hour corporate training workshops (total of 236 participants) were tested by the assessment and taught using the S/SC methods of teaching. Three six-hour corporate training workshops not using the assessment (total of thirty-four participants) and its teaching methods were given. Each workshop class was pre- and post-tested for content using identical questions and scoring. The difference in the individuals' test scores in the pre- and post-tests were the measurements used to compare the results of the experiment's two types of workshops. The result is as follows:

t = 3.08, p ≤ 0.05 (significant difference)

3. In Boston, MA, Growth Associates gave twenty-seven two-and-one-half-hour workshops for businesspeople (total of 683 participants). The participants were given the assessment, tested for content, taught using the S/SC methods of instruction and then re-tested for content. Five similar workshops (similar content and a total of sixty-seven businesspeople), were given the assessment, were identically pre-tested and post-tested for content and were taught not using the S/SC methods. The difference in the individuals' test scores in the pre- and post-tests were the measurements used to compare the results of the experiment's two groups. The result is as follows:

t = 3.23, p ≤ 0.05 (significant difference)

4. Forty-seven certification teaching courses, certified by the State Department of Education, Augusta, ME were given to educators consisting of seventeen to forty-six participants. The educators were given the assessment the first class and during the next two classes they were taught by the S/SC methods for teaching. Twelve control classes were given the assessment the first class but were taught without using the S/SC as a method of teaching. All classes were pre- and post-tested for content using identical questions and scoring. The difference in the individuals' test scores in the pre- and post-tests were the measurements used to compare the results of the experiment's two classes. The result is as follows:

t = 2.99, p ≤ 0.05 (significant difference)

5. Eighty-three engineers, sales, customer service and business people in one company (Security Plastics, Inc.) were tested using the assessment. Then, they were placed into specific jobs, put on teams and given certain supervisors based on their S/SC and the criteria of the role process and team process fit for their position. The performance measures of success and satisfaction for all of the study's participants after one year were measured using a verbal Likert scale (1-7) with a success polarity of "extremely productive" to "ready to be fired" and a satisfaction polarity of "love my work" to "hate my work" or had left their position because they were promoted or didn't like what they were doing. Ninety-four other employees were tested using the assessment and were placed

into jobs, on teams and with supervisors by using the company's usual methods. They and their supervisors were also given the verbal Likert scales. The Likert scale scores were the criteria used to demonstrate the following t-test results:

Placement satisfaction by employee: $t = 3.22$, $p \leq 0.05$*

Placement success by employee: $t = 2.91$, $p \leq 0.05$*

Placement success by the supervisor: $t = 3.14$, $p \leq 0.05$*

Placement satisfaction observed by the supervisor: $t = 3.43$, $p \leq 0.05$*
   *statistically significant difference

6. Forty-one employees (twenty-nine of this sample were college students) at two stores of a national copy chain (Kinko's of South Florida) were: given the assessment; evaluated for overall job performance by doing each of their rotating tasks during a shift; and evaluated for job performance by doing the rotating task that the S/SC phases predicts would be the highest performance criteria. An overall rotating task performance was measured by the supervisor evaluating each employee with a verbal Likert (1-7: Failing Performance — Excellent Performance). Overall job performance was measured by averaging all the rotating task scores together. The result of comparing the employees' productivity doing the overall tasks and their doing the S/SC predictive tasks follow:

$t = 2.34$, $p \leq 0.05$ (significant difference)

7. During a three-year period at Security Plastics, Inc., in Miami Lakes, FL, 346 adults were placed on sixty-eight teams. Forty-seven teams were formed using S/SC input data and twenty-one teams were done without using S/SC input data. The performance of these two different types of teams were measured by the individual team leaders using a verbal Likert scale (1-7: 1 = failing and 7 = excellent). The statistical comparison of these differently formed teams was done by a t-test.

$t = 3.16$, $p \leq 0.05$ (significant difference)

A more practical result was that the stores' percent of turnover dropped 34% during the three months that employees spent 80% of their time on the S/SC tasks and 20% rotating.

Generalizability

This topic is under study for the total underlying population. Early results yield an underlying multivariate normal distribution. The assessment is based on non-parametric methods but does yield indications that the resulting distribution is multivariate normal, which is common in the social and behavioral sciences.

Summary

The 5 Dynamics Assessment has been administered to more than 60,000 clients in the past twenty-eight years with close to 90% overall validity and reliability. The validity and reliability have been measured by numerous methods, inclusive of face validity in business and educational applications, substantive and structural validity, temporal reliability and form equivalence, internal consistency, construct and content validity and external validity.